Options on Atonement in Christian Thought

Options
on
Atonement
in
Christian Thought

Stephen Finlan

A Michael Glazier Book

LITURGICAL PRESS
Collegeville, Minnesota

www.litpress.org

A Michael Glazier Book published by Liturgical Press

Cover design by David Manahan, o.s.b. Illustration: color etching from *Passion* by Georges Rouault, published by Dover.

1   2   3   4   5   6   7   8

Library of Congress Cataloging-in-Publication Data

Finlan, Stephen.
    Options on atonement in Christian thought / Stephen Finlan.
        p.   cm.
    Includes bibliographical references and index.
    ISBN 978-0-8146-5986-1
        1. Atonement.   I. Title.

    BT265.3.F56 2007
    232'.3—dc22

                                                          2006038562

Contents

Abbreviations

AARA—American Academy of Religion Academy series

AB—Anchor Bible

Ac Bib—Academia Biblica

B.C.E.—Before the Common Era (= B.C.)

CBQ—Catholic Biblical Quarterly

C.E.—Common Era (= A.D.)

ETL—Ephemerides theologicae lovanienses

ExpT—Expository Times

FBBS—Facet Books, Biblical Series

HNT—Handbuch zum Neuen Testament

ICC—International Critical Commentary

JBL—Journal of Biblical Literature

JSJSup—*Journal for the Study of Judaism*, Supplement Series

JSNTSup—*Journal for the Study of the New Testament*, Supplement Series

JSOTSup—*Journal for the Study of the Old Testament*, Supplement Series

LXX—The Septuagint, the Greek translation of the Old Testament

NPNF 2—Nicene and Post-Nicene Fathers, second series

NT—New Testament

OT—Old Testament

PTMS—Princeton Theological Monographs Series

SBLDS—Society of Biblical Literature Dissertation Series

SBLSP—Society of Biblical Literature Seminar Papers

SJT—Scottish Journal of Theology

TDNT—Theological Dictionary of the New Testament

Introduction

What Is Atonement?

A wide range of ideas has received the label "atonement." For some it means providing some kind of gift or apology in order to repair a damaged relationship. For others such repair (if it is to be called atonement) must mean making a costly payment or enduring a painful ordeal. In either view the goal of atonement is reconciliation between persons. Reconciliation is also revealed in the etymology of the English word "atonement," a manufactured word derived from "at-one-ment."

But when we speak of atonement in connection with biblical studies and Christian doctrine we are referring to concepts of the saving power of the death of Jesus developed in the early Greek-speaking churches and developed further over the centuries in works written in Latin and other languages. When I speak of "atonement" I am referring to this group of meanings and doctrines we inherit from the early church.

The apostle Paul is the principal spokesman (in our surviving records) for these atonement concepts. He communicates them through cultic[1] and social metaphors he uses at key moments in his arguments. Six fundamental metaphors are drawn together (in varying combinations) to speak of atonement. Some picture the death of Jesus, some describe the beneficial effects on believers, and some can cover both. These six basic metaphors are sacrifice, scapegoat, redemption, justification, reconciliation, and adoption. I pause to define just one of these terms now. "Redemption"[2] (Greek *apolytrōsis* in Rom 3:24; 8:23; 1 Cor 1:30; Col 1:14) refers

---

[1] "Cult" refers to shared ritual, not to "extremist sect," despite the usage in popular media. *Every* religious community has a cultic practice that communicates the values and reinforces the social boundaries of the group. The centerpiece of the Jewish cult was animal sacrifice, which was used to cleanse impurity, some of which was believed to be caused by sin. The scapegoat rite was also an important part of the cult.

[2] NRSV is my default translation.

to the purchasing of a slave, to the paying of a manumission price to free a slave, or to the ransoming of hostages.[3] A redemption payment, then, could be lifesaving.

Paul would frequently combine two or three of these images in one sentence, allowing each metaphor to inform and help interpret the other. Underlying all the metaphors is the notion that Jesus died as a martyr. The Greeks called this kind of death a "noble death." This is not a metaphor, since noble death/martyrdom always refers to the violent death of a noble human being; its meaning is not changed when it is applied to the death of Jesus. On the other hand, the meanings of sacrifice, scapegoat, and redemption are *changed* when they are applied to Jesus' death; he was not *literally* a sacrificial animal, a banished goat, or a sum of money: these are metaphors.

Paul and his audience share the belief that Jesus died as a martyr. Paul then uses three metaphors (sacrifice, scapegoat, redemption) to interpret the martyrdom and employs four to describe believers' changed status (redemption, justification, reconciliation, adoption). Obviously the redemption metaphor is doing double duty.

Paul combines these metaphors in a variety of ways. A number of composite concepts have developed, and they continue to evolve and re-form to this day. Christians today hold many different ideas of atonement, though they often fail to notice these differences, not to mention the different components that came together to form the ideas. Some of the more common composite concepts are these:

1. Humanity had a huge debt of sin and was going to be condemned; Jesus agreed to suffer the penalty that humanity deserved and, because of his incomparable goodness, his death paid off all of humanity's sin-debt;

2. Jesus volunteered to take on human sin, allowing himself to become a lightning rod for the condemnation and wrath of God, and by so doing he actually carried away the sin and its associated penalty;

3. The sacrifices and other cleansing rituals of the OT cult all prefigured and pointed at the Messiah's self-sacrificial death, but his was the only death that *really* brought about the cleansing of conscience that the cult was thought to accomplish.

---

[3] Timothy Gorringe, "Title and Metaphor in Christology," *ExpT* 95 (1983–84) 9; James D. G. Dunn, *The Theology of Paul the Apostle* (Grand Rapids: Eerdmans, 1998) 227.

Each one of these is a composite concept, combining two or three ideas into a unique notion of atonement. Some idea of substitution is present in each of these concepts. The elements that explain *how* that substitution works in each of these cases are, respectively,

1. *A combined judicial-commercial-moral idea:* Sin incurs judicial guilt, and such guilt is comparable to a debt. The underlying metaphor within a metaphor is that guilt equals debt, while innocence has value, like a commercial value. The innocence of Jesus and the punishment he endured were sufficient to serve our penalty, pay our debt, and restore the moral balance sheet. In this metaphor innocent suffering is legal tender. Innocent suffering has excess power, *transferable* power.

2. *A combined judicial-scapegoat idea:* Sin arouses God's wrath; Jesus agrees to become the scapegoat who will receive the outpouring of that wrath, and in his death he *bears away* the sin and its penalty as the goat bore away the sins of the community. Actually, the judicial element is somewhat subdued because it is the *personal* wrath of God that is emphasized.

3. *A combined cultic sacrificial-moral idea:* Here the death fits into a ritual pattern. The *physical* purity of a spotless animal is equated with the *spiritual* purity of the righteous Messiah. Because of his purity status the Messiah's death has ritual effectiveness: the power to cleanse sins. The death of God's chosen one has a vicarious cleansing power that the animal sacrifices did not have, since they were only *physically* pure. This is the ruling concept in the letter to the Hebrews; it is only dimly present, if at all, in Paul.

The closer we look at what Christians understand atonement to be, the greater the diversity and complexity we observe. Even an apparently simple idea like "Jesus died for my sins" turns out to have many possible interpretations: he died heroically; more than that, he died as a penal substitute; beyond that, he *won* something for me through that death; he took on something and carried it away. This combines the imagery of the battlefield, the courtroom, and judicial execution.

In the oldest Christian texts (the letters of Paul) we see a number of images that speak of salvation achieved by a kind of *transaction* taking place at the cross, a penalty-bearing, a debt-canceling, or a redemption-purchasing. Similar ideas are common in several other NT epistles and in Revelation, yet they are almost completely absent from the gospels. The idea of "Christ dying for our sins" was not the emphasis of the Jerusalem church,[4] but before long it became the dominant teaching in the Gentile churches. At several key points in Christian history certain theologians formulated concepts of atonement that took the metaphors quite literally and ignored other aspects of Paul's theology, such as the spiritual transformation of believers.

Atonement was separated from and given precedence over other biblical images of salvation. Further, these concepts of atonement were detached from the vitality of personal religious experience and turned into dogmas, taking on a life of their own. For most Christians the notion of substitutionary atonement is encountered not in biblical sayings but in popular formulas that heighten the harsher elements. Many grew up believing that salvation meant a violent rescue from the threatened violence of an angry God. Such fear-based thinking is quite distant from the gospel teaching "fear not" (Luke 5:10; 12:32, KJV).

Harsh and Violent Formulations of Atonement

Many Christians are eager to know what their options are for reacting to and assessing the various atonement teachings they hear. Many are having difficulty understanding a supposed divine law of justice that demanded a verdict but was so unjust as to allow the substitution of an innocent victim in place of the guilty. Even more difficult to accept is the notion of God (or "justice") being paid off. Perhaps these metaphors were not meant to be taken as literally as theologians have taken them. More recently, different responses to atonement are being heard. These say that God was not persuaded in any way; rather, God, *in* Jesus, was participating in human suffering, proving that violence was ultimately powerless or showing us how deeply involved we are in collective violence directed against chosen victims. Perhaps the metaphor was never meant to speak of a change in God's attitude but only to change the human tendency to commit, and to lie about, violence.

Many Christians are reassessing what they were taught as children, that "Jesus was killed for you." They are questioning what they were told as teenagers, that only the intercession of the tortured Messiah could rescue them from eternal torture at the hands of a "loving" God. Many are no longer convinced by what they currently hear from the pulpit, that God could not just forgive and forget, that *someone* had to take on

[4] Douglas A. Hare, *The Son of Man Tradition* (Minneapolis: Fortress Press, 1990) 276–77.

the penalty of sin. They no longer see any sense in the notion of forgiveness being gained through a misdirection of the punishing wrath of God onto his innocent son. What kind of "father" would make forgiveness conditional upon such an act? Have we failed to appreciate the profoundly ethical and intimate implications of calling God "father," or is this an abusive and fear-driven father?

Many Christians find it hard to accept Saint Anselm's idea that sin did damage to God's honor and that Christ's death was a "recompense for the injury."[5] They are no longer convinced by Calvin's notion that "He by his death purchased life for us" as "a payment or compensation which acquits us from guilt."[6]

Such theology may indeed draw upon Paul's, but there are other themes in his teaching that should prevent the harsh and transactional elements from dominating. Further, Paul initiates a spiritualizing pattern that will be followed by most of his successors, wherein the violent implications of atonement are somewhat downplayed while the generosity of God and the transformation of believers into the likeness of God are stressed.

But popular Christian beliefs often have nothing to do with spiritual progress and transformation, focusing instead upon crude ideas of Jesus' death as a payoff, a sacrifice, a punishment-bearing, for "Jesus took the hit for me"; "Jesus bled and died for me"; "that should have been me up on the cross."

Many theologians, ancient and contemporary, have not been happy with expressions of a violent and judicial God and have sought to constrain, spiritualize, or minimize these concepts, even denying that a payment-demanding God was ever envisioned. Some of them, however, retain the vocabulary and logic of sacrifice, though sentimentalizing it. A smaller group of thinkers has ceased to speak of the death of Jesus as any kind of purchase or transaction with God, focusing instead on the lessons to be learned from Jesus' life and character, which *includes* his courageous stance in the face of death.

This is a good place to raise the subject of progressive development in religious conceptualization, progress both within and outside the Bible. One can witness the development of religious ideas within the Bible,

---

[5] Anselm of Canterbury, *Cur Deus Homo?* 1.11, trans. Edward S. Prout (London: Religious Tract Society, 1887) 64.

[6] Jean Calvin, *Institutes of the Christian Religion* 2.16.7; 17.7, trans. Henry Beveridge (Grand Rapids: Eerdmans, 1975) 1:440, 457.

with later parts of the Bible even critiquing or "correcting" the earlier parts: Chronicles corrects Kings; Micah and Jeremiah reject the sacrificial cult; Jesus asks for deeper devotion than the Torah demanded; Paul says the old covenant has a fading glory while the new covenant has a permanent glory.

How does our understanding of God grow, and can we gain new insight into the relevant biblical passages by revisiting them? How did atonement ideas come to play such an important role, and what do we make of them now? These are questions I will address in the course of this work. Further, there is much to be gained from a reexamination of what led to the crucifixion and what we can learn from Jesus' attitude.

How have theologians and preachers handled the old ideas of Jesus' death as ritual purification or as redemption payment? I see the proposed solutions falling mostly into three categories: primitivizing, spiritualizing, and rejecting. One group affirms the primitive and violent ideas; another group tries to scrub them clean, downplaying the divine violence in them; the third rejects all notions of salvation through redemption payment or ritual death. Readers must decide which of these options fits best with Jesus' own emphasis on straightforward trust in God and honesty in dealings with people. The most commonly occurring option is the second one. The creativity of the various strategies for rescuing, rationalizing, and redefining atonement is really quite remarkable. It enables theologians to avoid facing the fact that the problems with atonement are present in our Scriptures; it is easier to say that all difficulties lie in a misinterpretation or distortion of the Scriptures, which is, after all, *largely* true. But contradictory messages can be found even in the same biblical author, such as the notion of God being both violent and forgiving, and of salvation being both "free"[7] and "purchased."[8]

It is necessary to look now at the lineage of atonement-related ideas and practices in Judaism, and then move on to the apostle Paul, who constructed his atonement metaphors from ritual and social practices in Jewish and Gentile societies. Later I will examine a number of particular options on atonement, finishing with a discussion of spiritual growth and religious philosophic progress.

---

[7] Rom 5:15-17; 6:23; 2 Cor 3:17; Gal 5:1, 13.
[8] 1 Cor 6:20; 7:23; Acts 20:28.

The Roots of Atonement

1.1 Holiness

Atonement draws on a number of ancient religious concepts. One is "holiness," which signifies separation, the necessary distance between the profanely human and the awesomely divine. "Holiness" did not originally have a moralized meaning but spoke of a necessary separation of what is common from what is holy, *qodesh*, as when the Israelites are told not to set foot on the holy Mount Sinai (Exod 19:12), a notion retained even in the NT: "You have not come to something that can be touched, a blazing fire, and darkness, and gloom, and a tempest" (Heb 12:18). This shows the threatening and frightening aspect of the holy. "Set limits" (Exod 19:12) is the watchword of religion at this level of development; the purity code sets strict limits everywhere.

The enforcement of boundaries (spiritual and social) is the essence of purity systems. Ritual both enforces and crosses these boundaries according to strictly controlled procedures interpreted by the sacred technicians, the priests. Ritual assumes a highly structured universe and supports a highly structured society. Everyone is expected to conform to certain purity codes and procedures, but the priests are subject to many more purity restrictions because they have access to the realm of the Holy.

Transgression, the crossing of boundaries, means danger, retaliation, and penalty. Actually a limited penalty is welcomed, since paying it mollifies the deity's wrath. The alternative is death. Numinous awe and danger surround ritual objects: Nadab and Abihu offer up "unauthorized coals"[1] and are blasted by the Lord (Lev 10:1-2). In the case of a man who

---

[1] Jacob Milgrom's translation; the NRSV and most modern translations have "unholy fire" (cf. KJB: "strange fire"). They probably brought them from a profane source instead

innocently reached out to steady the ark of the covenant, "the anger of the LORD was kindled against Uzzah; and God struck him there" (2 Sam 6:7). When King Uzziah "became angry with the priests a leprous disease broke out on his forehead" (2 Chr 26:19). Even complaining can provoke the Lord to lash out and burn up some parts of the camp (Num 11:1). God is "a devouring fire" (Exod 24:17; Deut 5:22) who sends flames down to consume his enemies (2 Kgs 1:10-12), even "consum[ing] . . . two hundred fifty men" on one occasion (Num 16:35). This last is a violent "reminder . . . that no [one] who is not of the descendants of Aaron, shall approach to offer incense" (Num 16:40). Priestly space is protected with stories of unlimited violence.

Concerns about the evil or dangerous moods of gods come from a very primitive level of religious psychology. The strategies of aversion, placation, propitiation, and deception have frequently been associated with sacrificial rituals. As notions of uncleanness and sin develop over long periods of time, however, they give evidence of moral reflection and display a gradually expanding trust in the reliability of the spirit forces. The deity's wrath is increasingly seen to be motivated mainly against injustice and cruelty and less against ritual infractions. Different levels of religious conceptualization are evidenced by the debates within religious traditions, when those who aspire for higher ethical levels criticize the ritualism and political favoritism manifested by those on lower ethical levels.

1.2 The Metaphysics of Sacrifice

A Food Payment

Since atonement builds on sacrificial theology, one of the roots of atonement lies in the ancient idea of actually feeding the god with the smoke of the burning animal, strongly attested in the first four books of the Pentateuch.[2] The priests' job is to "offer the LORD's offerings by fire, the food of their God . . . the food of your God" (Lev 21:6, 8). YHWH demands "the food for my offerings by fire, my pleasing odor" (Num 28:2).

---

of from the sacrificial altar (Jacob Milgrom, *Leviticus 1–16*. AB 3 [Garden City: Doubleday, 1991] 598).

[2] Milgrom says feeding God is "not to be found in Israel"—and promptly goes on to admit that feeding God was "the original aim" of table, bread, altar, and candelabrum and that evidence of it is found "in some sacrificial idioms of the Bible: 'my table' (Ezek 44:15), 'the food of his God' ([Lev] 21:22)" (*Leviticus 1–16*, 440).

This wording can even be seen in the NT in Ephesians 5:2, where Christ's sacrifice is a "fragrant offering" in the nostrils of God. Of course, in Ephesians this is metaphoric, but such metaphor rests on and reinterprets primitive beliefs.

Hebrew sacrifice had more than one purpose and was supported by more than one metaphysical belief. The most important sacrifice in the preexilic period was the burnt offering, which sends up to God a "soothing aroma" (NASB) or "pleasing odor" (NRSV). The "soothing" meaning is seen in the verb root *nwch* (in the Qal, *nāchāh*), which signifies "rest."[3] The pleasing odor (*reyach nichoach*) is mentioned thirty-nine times in the Pentateuch and three times in Ezekiel. It is a pacifying aroma, mollifying God: "when the LORD smelled the pleasing odor, the LORD said in his heart, 'I will never again curse the ground because of humankind'" (Gen 8:21).[4] Whole offerings, sometimes accompanied by peace offerings (as in 2 Sam 24:25) were "occasionally offered to propitiate the wrath of Jahweh, especially in times of crisis."[5] In the postexilic period, when crude propitiatory concepts are partially replaced by ideas of cleansing, the sin offering and guilt offering become the most important sacrifices. (See the next subsection.)

"Propitiation" is a term often used by scholars to designate this business of appeasing someone who is angry. Propitiating the deity was probably the original role for sacrifice in all sacrificing cultures. Sacrifice as payment is clearly seen in much of the OT. The sacrifice must be costly to be effective; something received as a gift cannot function as a sacrifice (2 Sam 24:24).

Scholars are fairly straightforward in admitting the frankly selfish motive of ancient sacrifice; it is "a gift to the deity to induce his aid."[6] For some reason, however, they rarely focus on the fact that these gifts are the culture's most valuable *food* commodities, with an emphasis on costly meat: offerings are "the food of your God" (Lev 21:8). Sacrifice is like a tribute payment to an emperor: God demands that "no one shall

[3] William L. Holladay, *A Concise Hebrew and Aramaic Lexicon of the Old Testament* (Grand Rapids: Eerdmans, 1988) 231, meanings 2 through 4.

[4] The "rest-giving smell . . . quiets the anger of Yahweh or placates him" (George Buchanan Gray, *Sacrifice in the Old Testament: Its Theory and Practice* [Oxford: Clarendon Press, 1925] 77).

[5] Frances M. Young, *The Use of Sacrificial Ideas in Greek Christian Writers from the New Testament to John Chrysostom*. Patristic Monograph Series 2 (Eugene, OR: Wipf & Stock, 1979) 39, with n. 23.

[6] Milgrom, *Leviticus 1–16*, 441.

appear before me empty-handed" (Exod 23:15). In ancient times the food was thought to *strengthen* the deity, an anthropomorphic notion that is only partially suppressed by the biblical redactors.

Cleansing

Sacrifice-as-food-payment is not the end of the story, of course. Even within the Pentateuch we see what looks like an ongoing argument about the purpose of sacrifice. The naturalistic idea of God's anger being soothed with a food payment is the understanding in parts of Genesis (J, the Yahwist author), Samuel, and Kings. But the Pentateuchal author/redactor called "P" (for priestly) does not care for the idea of sacrifice as food payment. In its place P develops a complex metaphysics of ritual cleansing or purging impurity that is literal, not metaphorical, and poses a spiritual threat to the community. Sacrifice, for P, is not meant for appeasement but for obtaining a spiritually cleansing substance: blood. The blood obtained from the *ḥattaʾt* ("sin offering," KJV, NRSV; "purification offering," Milgrom) is used to cleanse various installations in the Temple where impurity has lodged.

Sin committed anywhere in Israel pollutes the Temple, attaching to it like a "miasma."[7] More serious sin, or sin committed by priests, seeps in further, even to the curtain separating the Holy Place from the Most Holy Place. Deliberate sin penetrates all the way into the Most Holy Place, to the lid of the ark of the covenant, which is the mercy seat (*kapporet* in Hebrew; *hilastērion* in Greek).[8] Impurity from lesser sins, and sins committed by lesser persons, can be cleansed at any time; every Sabbath the priests conduct sacrifice and apply the sacrificial blood to the horns of the outer altar and the incense altar, expunging involuntary sin and lesser impurities.

Sins committed "with a high hand" and sins committed by the priests, however, are not removed by these routine sacrifices; the ark of the covenant retains the pollution from these acts, and it must be removed annually or God will abandon the Temple. Cleansing this impurity requires the sprinkling of *ḥattaʾt* blood on the *kapporet* in the Most Holy Place, a

---

[7] Samuel E. Balentine, *Leviticus*. Interpretation (Louisville: Westminster John Knox, 2002) 128–29.

[8] Jacob Milgrom, "The Priestly Laws of Sancta Contamination," in Michael Fishbane and Emanuel Tov, eds., *"Shaʾarei Talmon": Studies in the Bible, Qumran, and the Ancient Near East Presented to Shemaryahu Talmon* (Winona Lake: Eisenbrauns, 1992) 142–43.

ritual performed only once a year, on the Day of Atonement.[9] The Day of Atonement, then, in Milgrom's understanding, is more correctly the Day of Purification.[10]

Milgrom has shown that the principal Hebrew sacrifices are a matter of Temple purification, not of substitutionary death. It is a Christianizing distortion to say that the animal's death is a substitutionary punishment or that the blood takes on the stain of sin. Rather, it is the *Temple* that has been corrupted, and blood is a *cleanser.*[11] Sacrifice was propitiatory for J but was protective and cleansing for P (the Priestly author), whose ideology dominates Second Temple practice. H (for "Holiness Code") combines these views (see below). The D (Deuteronomist) author is mainly concerned with the question of covenant loyalty, caring little about cultic metaphysics as long as there is only one Temple (in Jerusalem).

Payment and Aversion

The fundamental term for purging or cleansing, *kipper,* was not an exclusively sacrificial term, but it was inextricably linked to the idea of a payoff. *Kipper* (atonement) is cognate with *kopher.* A *kopher* is a payment, specifically a "payment for the redemption of forfeited life."[12] It is "a ransom for their lives . . . atonement money" (Exod 30:12, 15, 16), an "atonement" in the form of "articles of gold, armlets and bracelets" (Num 31:50), a way of averting someone's wrath, either humans', as in Genesis 32:20 ("I may appease him with the present") and Proverbs 16:14 ("a king's wrath . . . appease it"); or Yhwh's, as in Numbers 8:19 (averting punishment for encroachment on sacred territory) and Exodus 32:30 (trying to persuade God not to lash out after the golden calf incident).

This is not just a restoration of propriety; it is an aversion of human or divine violence. Violence is highlighted in some of the non-ritual usages of *kipper,* where a murderer is the *kipperer.* God is frankly appeased

---

[9] Frank H. Gorman Jr., *The Ideology of Ritual: Space, Time and Status in the Priestly Theology.* JSOTSup 91 (Sheffield: Sheffield Academic Press, 1990) 74–84.

[10] Milgrom is sometimes rigid on this point, claiming that sacrifice does *not* secure forgiveness for sinners, but *only* cleanses the sanctuary (*Leviticus 1–16*, 254–55). John Dennis is one of a number of scholars who point out that both cleansing and forgiveness are taking place ("The Function of the *ḥṭʾt* Sacrifice in the Priestly Literature" [*ETL* 78 (2002) 112, 115–18, 121]).

[11] Stephen Finlan, *The Background and Content of Paul's Cultic Atonement Metaphors.* Ac Bib 19 (Atlanta: SBL/Brill, 2004) 32–35, 38, 41–42.

[12] Leon Morris, *The Apostolic Preaching of the Cross.* 3rd rev. ed. (Grand Rapids: Eerdmans, 1965) 161–62.

by the "righteous" violence (Ps 106:31) of the priest Phinehas, who drove his spear through a Hebrew man and a Midianite woman while they were in the act of lovemaking. Yhwh was prepared to destroy the whole nation until the priestly killer "made atonement for the Israelites" (Num 25:13)—or "interceded," in the euphemism of the psalm (106:30)—with this act of violence, which successfully "turned back my wrath from the Israelites" (Num 25:11). Even more gruesome is the atrocious "making expiation" (*kipper,* 2 Sam 21:3) that David does to the Gibeonites by handing over seven relatives of Saul to be impaled or crucified on a city wall. Yhwh was even involved in the early part of this last event, having informed David that there was blood-guilt on Saul's house (21:1). All of this shows us the undercurrent of violence in *kipper,* something the P editor tried to spiritualize out of the picture, describing instead a sure procedure for repeated cleansing of the constantly accumulating impurity of Israel, suppressing the fact that this act had been thought to avert the anger of Yhwh.

The next Pentateuchal author, H (for "Holiness Code"), is not content with an impersonal cleansing process; he repersonalizes the cult. H is taking more literally the idea that sacrificial odors are literally "pleasing," are even a kind of payment.[13] H is the author of the central "explanatory" verse:

> For the life of the flesh is in the blood; and I have given it to you for making atonement for your lives on the altar; for, as life, it is the blood that makes atonement. (Lev 17:11)

However, the idea of blood, *as life,* being able to make atonement is hardly a clear explanation to modern people. The logic is either that the life force in the blood can cleanse the anti-life force that is impurity, or that the animal's life is a payment or substitute "for your lives" (17:11), a notion that is not present in P. Thus there can be a dual meaning in H. In either case the sacrifice has literal value; it is not just a symbol enacted to dramatize cleansing or gift giving; it is *literally* cleansing (P and H) or gift giving (J and H).

Doing *kipper*, then, means conciliating, placating, wiping clean, or paying off. The ritual assumes an environment of potential divine violence and a remedy based on either placation or magic. Whichever meta-

---

[13] Israel Knohl, "The Sin Offering Law in the 'Holiness School,'" in Gary A. Anderson and Saul M. Olyan, eds., *Priesthood and Cult in Ancient Israel.* JSOTSup 125 (Sheffield: Sheffield Academic Press, 1991) 203.

physics is dominant in the minds of particular practitioners, the ritual is manipulative. Whether one thinks to give the Lord goods that he desires, or whether one believes in the efficacy of manipulating a spiritual substance (blood), the thinking is manipulative. In neither case is atonement connected with moral decision or reform, though in the late Second Temple period repentance finally came to be considered essential to the efficacy of sacrifice. A ritual that started with naturalistic metaphysics took on ethical meaning. The priests had assimilated the ideas of the prophets.

Completely different from these other sacrifices, and having nothing to do with cleansing, forgiveness, or reparation, was the Passover sacrifice. The reiterated Passover was commemorative (of the Exodus from Egypt), but its original function (within the Exodus story) was apotropaic: warding away the Angel of Death who was out to kill all the firstborn in the land. Yet for Paul even this was suggestive of Jesus' saving death: "for our paschal lamb, Christ, has been sacrificed" (1 Cor 5:7).

1.3 The Scapegoat Ritual

Another violent cultic image is that of the expulsion ritual, of which the best known is the scapegoat in the Hebrew cult. Scapegoat ritual is to be distinguished from sacrifice, even though the former took place at the same time as the most important sacrifices, the *ḥaṭṭaʾt* offerings of the Day of Atonement. The scapegoat ritual is surrounded by the regime of sacrificial cleansings (Lev 16), yet retains its distinctive character: an expulsion ritual, not a sacrifice. It is not an offering, not a cleansing, not even something that has much to do with the Deity. It is a very ancient and naturalistic rite, literally carrying away sin, not impurity.[14] Sin is literally *"put . . .* on the head of the goat," and "the goat shall *bear* on itself all their iniquities to a barren region" (Lev 16:21-22, emphasis added). Furthermore, this goat is ritually maltreated—its hair is pulled, it is cursed, pierced, spat upon,[15] things that are never done to a sacrificial animal. Scapegoat is a very ancient rite of naturalistic (literal) sin expulsion, one where the Deity's attitude is not mentioned, nor need it be. If

---

[14] Milgrom, *Leviticus 17–22*. AB 3A (Garden City: Doubleday, 2000) 2445.

[15] Mishnah, *Yoma* 6:4; *Barnabas* 7:6-8; Tertullian, *Adv. Marcion* 3.7.7; Daniel Stökl Ben Ezra, *The Impact of Yom Kippur on Early Christianity: The Day of Atonement from Second Temple Judaism to the Fifth Century.* WUNT 163 (Tübingen: Mohr Siebeck, 2003) 31 n. 70, 152–53, 157–59.

sin can be literally transported, what does the Deity's attitude matter? Sacrifice is much more theologically advanced than expulsion ritual, because the Deity's attitude *is* relevant in sacrificial ritual. The detailed instructions about handling sacrificial blood act out the community's worshipful concepts of holiness, pollution, cleansing, and obeisance. The scapegoat ritual is not an act of worship but a violent act of self-defense based on the most primitive metaphysics.

There was also a long tradition of expulsion rituals in popular Greek culture, particularly the practice of selecting and expelling a *pharmakos*, a "medicinal." The *pharmakos* was a human victim, sometimes a prisoner, who was selected, ritually abused, and chased away from the city, carrying away a disease or impurity.[16] This was a well-known practice and a vivid image during Paul's time, even if its actual practice was disappearing.

1.4 Internalization or Spiritualization

In cultures from Asia to Europe to Africa there is a progressive and observable development away from violent sacrificial practices toward a concentration on ethics and an increased valuation of the individual's spiritual motive, a process that can be called spiritualization. The sacrificer "sacrifices only in himself,"[17] says an Indian text, while Jewish texts say God wants the sacrifice of a "contrite heart" or of "thanksgiving" more than an "ox or a bull" (Pss 51:16-17; 50:12-14; 69:30-31). This can be called "interiorized" or "internal" sacrifice.[18] In this kind of spiritualization[19] motive is everything: the *true* sacrifice is not the ritual act but the inward disposition.

Others, such as Hosea, Micah, Jeremiah, and Plato, have preferred to openly attack sacrifice and the manipulative motives with which it is practiced, mocking or condemning the institution rather than advocating reform,[20] although some scholars try to turn these prophets into mere

---

[16] Martin Hengel, *The Atonement: The Origins of the Doctrine in the New Testament* (London: SCM, 1981) 24–27; Gustav Stählin, περίψημα, *TDNT* 6:84–87.

[17] Maitri Upanishad 6.9; Brian K. Smith, *Reflections on Resemblance, Ritual, and Religion* (Oxford: Oxford University Press, 1989) 209.

[18] J. C. Heesterman, *The Inner Conflict of Tradition: Essays in Indian Ritual, Kingship, and Society* (Chicago: University of Chicago Press, 1985) 39, 42, 213 n. 77, 214 n. 88.

[19] I refer to internalization as Level Three spiritualization, among the six levels of spiritualization I discern (Finlan, *Background and Content*, 49–50, 60–61; idem, *Problems with Atonement: The Origins of, and Controversy about, the Atonement Doctrine* [Collegeville: Liturgical Press, 2005] 22–23).

[20] Hos 4:8; 6:6; 8:11-12; 10:2; Mic 6:6-8; Jer 7:22-23; Plato, *Laws* 10.885C; 10.909B, 948C.

reformers or even Temple employees. *Some* certainly *were* reformers and thus defenders of the Temple institution (such as Ezekiel, Joel, and Malachi) and some undoubtedly were not (such as Amos, Micah, Jeremiah, and the authors of Isaiah 1 and Psalms 40, 50, and 51). In different ways, priests, scribes, and prophets engaged in various efforts to spiritualize, intellectualize, and interiorize the Hebrew cult.[21]

By the time of Paul, intellectuals among both the Greeks and the Jews had for centuries been critiquing, rethinking, and reinterpreting animal sacrifice, both by highlighting the inner attitude of the giver rather than the outward rite and by using sacrificial terminology metaphorically. Spiritualization shaped much Christian interpretation of the OT; violence in the text was often taken as a metaphor for spiritual struggle.

Spiritualization also ties in to the martyrological tradition. The Greek tragedians developed the idea of self-sacrifice for one's city or for a religious principle into a major literary/religious theme, using explicitly sacrificial terms. The Jews also wrote of the selfless suffering of a prophet or righteous one, particularly in Psalms 22:17, 25; 35:14; 69:9-14; Isaiah 53:3-10; Zechariah 12:10–13:9; Wisdom 2:10-24, using sacrificial imagery in some of these passages (Isa 53:10; Zech 13:1, for instance).

1.5 Cultic Labels for Noble Death

The idea of dying heroically for a cause, known as "noble death," was the most prominent dramatic theme in the works of the greatest playwrights of the Greek world, Sophocles and Euripides. Sometimes the death is seen as saving the nation or securing victory in war; in the great play *Antigone*, Sophocles' heroine dies for "the holiest laws of heaven"[22]— showing proper respect for the dead body, which is also important for the soul. Repeatedly these noble deaths (or martyrdoms, as we call them) are pictured as cultic acts. The heroine Iphigenia beseeches Zeus to "receive this sacrifice . . . the undefiled blood of a fair maiden's throat."[23] She dies for Greece: "I freely give on behalf of my own country. . . . Lead me to the altar to sacrifice."[24]

---

[21] Young, *Use of Sacrificial Ideas*, 57–63, 71.

[22] *Antigone*, approximately line 89, from *Sophocles: The Theban Plays*, trans. E. F. Watling (London: Penguin Books, 1947) 128.

[23] *Iph. aul.*, lines 1573–77; from *Ten Plays by Euripides*, trans. Moses Hadas and John McLean (New York: Bantam Books, 1960) 352.

[24] *Iph. aul.* 1553–55; from Hadas and McLean, *Ten Plays*, 352.

When the Romans adapt this idea it is generally in a military setting, taking the form of dedication to the gods of the underworld before going into a battle where they are doomed to die.[25] A family of famous military martyrs, the Decii, is mentioned by Roman authors of varying philosophical affiliations.

Jewish authors drew upon the noble death theme. Second Maccabees 6:18–7:42 is a lengthy narration of the torture and killing of a Jewish family who refused to scorn the Torah. The martyrs are confident that "God has [not] forsaken our people" but "will again be reconciled with his own servants" (7:16, 33). One hopes "through me and my brothers to bring to an end the wrath of the Almighty" (7:38).

The benefit secured by these deaths is made more explicit in *Fourth Maccabees*, which retells the story: "they vindicated their nation" (17:10); "by their endurance they conquered the tyrant" (1:11). Even a metaphor of purchase is used: their deaths acted as a "ransom" (17:21) or "exchange" (6:29) (*antipsychon* in both cases). Further, this book repeatedly attaches cultic terms to the deaths:

> Make my blood their purification (*katharsion*). (*4 Macc.* 6:29)

> The homeland [was] purified (*katharizō*) . . . through the blood of those devout ones and their atoning death[26] (*hilastēriou tou thanatou*)." (*4 Macc.* 17:21-22)

These create inevitable comparisons with Romans 3:25 and 1 Timothy 2:6, where the same (*haimati, hilastērion*) or similar (*antilytron*) words occur. Underlying all this heroism and self-sacrifice is the anger and violence of God ("he disciplines us with calamities"; "we are suffering because of our own sins. . . . Our living Lord is angry for a little while, to . . . discipline us," 2 Macc 6:16; 7:32-33). The deaths are vicariously beneficial to others ("let our punishment suffice for them. Make my blood their purification," 4 Macc. 6:28-29). The wrath of divine retribution hangs over the whole scene; martyrdom is a way to escape the wrath, even to appease the wrathful one, but it in no way challenges the concept of divine retribution. In fact, martyrdom inscribes and perpetuates the concept of a wrathful God.

The political component of martyrology is often highlighted. Muslim suicide bombers today understand their metaphorical sacrifices to be

---

[25] Jan Willem Van Henten, *The Maccabean Martyrs as Saviours of the Jewish People: A Study of 2 and 4 Maccabees.* JSJSup 57 (Leiden: Brill, 1997) 147.

[26] I change NRSV's inaccurate "death as an atoning sacrifice" to "atoning death."

"purchasing" them a place in Paradise. Christian Crusaders used the same rhetoric. Patriots of many nations speak of "sacred blood" and the "hallowed ground" where it was spilled. And where sacred blood has once been spilled, it is likely to be spilled again. Sites of worship, once Hindu and now Muslim, or vice versa, are the focus of many attacks in India. In sacrifice and sacrificial language, religious and political ideas come together, and violence is never far away. Spiritualization, then, is a limited blessing, partly uplifting, but partly covering over a failure to be uplifted.

2

Paul's Cultic Metaphors

Our oldest written sources of Christian atonement thinking are the letters of the apostle Paul. First we must note that Paul uses recognizable noble-death turns of phrase when he speaks of Christ dying "for us" (Rom 5:8), "for me" (Gal 2:20), "for the ungodly" (Rom 5:6), for "your brother or sister" (Rom 14:15). But what is the significance of this death? Why does it have a saving effect on others? This is where atonement ideas, as such, come in.

Paul claims that the Antioch Christians who instructed him in the gospel taught him that "Christ died for our sins in accordance with the scriptures" (1 Cor 15:3). The crucifixion is central to his proclamation: "I decided to know nothing among you except Jesus Christ, and him crucified" (1 Cor 2:2). Christ's action was heroic ("Christ died for us," Rom 5:8), it was due to human sin (he "was handed over to death for our trespasses," Rom 4:25), and it can be pictured as a sacrifice ("our Passover lamb, Christ, has been sacrificed," 1 Cor 5:7). These remarks of the Antioch-trained apostle seem to echo the themes of Antiochene martyrological literature (2 Maccabees and 4 *Maccabees*). Of course, Paul's theological vision will go far beyond anything found in the Maccabean literature.

2.1 Atonement in Romans

Paul's most important and developed theological statement is presented in the letter to the Romans. The first three chapters offer a lengthy description of humanity's problem—being hopelessly enslaved to sin. He finally reaches the solution in 3:24-30: Christ is our justification and redemption, since he was put forward as the new place of atonement in his blood, and God will justify anyone, Jew or Gentile, who has faith in Jesus. These are judicial, commercial, and ritual images for the efficacy of the death of Christ, picturing that death as bringing about acquittal, constituting a payment, or functioning as a cultic event. In later chapters Paul speaks of believers being reconciled or adopted, and these descriptions of the believer's radically changed social status should be considered a fourth area of metaphor. Let us look at each of these four in turn.

Our first major metaphor in Romans 3:24-26 is that believers are justified (cf. 4:25; 5:9; 8:1, 30). Justification literally means being "declared just" or "made just." In the context of the trial of the soul before God it means acquittal (being "declared just" in court). An important additional meaning, though, is the actual *making just* or change of character Paul envisages: believers become righteous and blameless; they are able to discern and do the will of God (Phil 1:9-10; Col 1:9, 22; 3:10;[1] 2 Cor 5:17, 21; Rom 12:2). Such character renewal, unfortunately, lies largely outside the scope of this book, but it is important to mention that justification or "rightwising"[2] has this dual meaning.

After the acquittal/justification arranged by Jesus, "Who will bring any charge against God's elect?" (Rom 8:33). Salvation, however, comes not just from what Jesus arranged but from *who he is*, namely, the divine Messiah and Son of God, and one needs to be connected to him. Paul's favorite term for this connection is "in Christ." Those who are so connected are acquitted, too: "There is therefore now no condemnation for those who are in Christ Jesus" (Rom 8:1). This acquittal ties in with Paul's longer discussions of law and condemnation (Rom 2; 3; 5; 8:1-4, 30-34, and elsewhere). The judicial aspect of justification has, however, been unduly raised to an all-dominating position by some scholars, when in fact it is just one of Paul's themes and does not explain the others, like spiritual rebirth, experiencing the presence of Christ, or being set free from the *power* of sin (not just its penalty).[3]

---

[1] I treat Colossians as Paul's. At the very least, the thought and expression are very close to Paul's, closer than is Ephesians. Some of the issues are addressed by Pheme Perkins ("God, Cosmos and Church Universal: The Theology of Ephesians," in *SBLSP* 2000 [Atlanta: Scholars Press, 2000] 754–55, 764–67), and Markus Bockmuehl (*Revelation and Mystery in Ancient Judaism and Pauline Christianity* [Grand Rapids: Eerdmans, 1997] 199).

[2] A term of Rudolf Bultmann's (*Theology of the New Testament* [New York: Charles Scribner's Sons, 1951] 1:272–87), who, unfortunately, denies any *actual* making good, any real character change, a conclusion that is justly criticized by Edgar J. Goodspeed ("Some Greek Notes," *JBL* 73 [1954] 87).

[3] Ably argued by Kari Kuula in *The Law, the Covenant and God's Plan*, vol. 2 of *Paul's Treatment of the Law and Israel in Romans* (Göttingen: Vandenhoeck & Ruprecht, 2003) 76.

Justification is "through the redemption that is in Christ Jesus" (3:24), so redemption is the second metaphor. Redemption (*apolytrōsis*) usually means the purchase of a slave's freedom, occasionally a ransom payment for the release of captives. Slaves in the Roman empire could make money and eventually purchase their own freedom. Obviously a metaphor that spoke of gaining one's freedom or gaining a kindly new owner would be a powerful one for any of Paul's readers who either had managed to purchase their freedom or who hoped to be able to do so in the future. Redemption, then, signifies a significant change of status.

Words related to *apolytrōsis*, particularly the verb *lytroomai* and the noun *lytron*, were used in the LXX to describe God's rescuing of Israel from Egypt,[4] for rescue in general,[5] or for the payment that redeems a firstborn son or animal from being sacrificed.[6] Some of Paul's audience may have thought of the *lytron* in Exodus when Paul spoke of *apolytrōsis*; Paul may have expected some of his metaphors to have a double resonance in his mixed audiences. Whichever echo is heard, the hearer would register the message of rescue by Jesus the Messiah (a phrase I will use periodically in order to emphasize that "Christ" is Greek for "Messiah," and that it still has this meaning for Paul).

Continuing the same sentence (but now in 3:25), Paul says Christ was put forward as *hilastērion*. The translation choices "place of atonement" (NRSV marginal translation) or "mercy seat" are preferable to "sacrifice of atonement" (NRSV, NIV) or "expiation" (NAB), which are inaccurate. Dan Bailey has shown that *hilastērion* is never translated "sacrificial victim" or "sacrificial ritual" in the LXX or other Greek literature. In the LXX *hilastērion* usually refers to the mercy seat in the wilderness tabernacle or in the Jerusalem Temple,[7] occasionally to a part of other temples.[8] In fact, whenever the word is connected with a temple it signifies the place where the action of the verb *hilaskomai* (appease, cleanse) or the verbal clause *hileōs genou* (be conciliated, be merciful) is accomplished. The act of ritual cleansing takes place on the *kapporet* (Hebrew) or

---

Kuula insists that the key to Paul's theology is his lived and shared religious *experience* "in Christ."

[4] Exod 15:13; Deut 9:26; 21:8; 2 Sam 7:23; Ps 77:15.

[5] 1 Kgs 1:29; Pss 31:5; 103:4; Isa 41:14; 52:3.

[6] Exod 13:13-15; 34:20; Num 18:15.

[7] Exod 25:17, 21, and nineteen other places in the Pentateuch, all meaning "mercy seat" (Daniel P. Bailey, "Jesus as the Mercy Seat: The Semantics and Theology of Paul's Use of *Hilastērion* in Romans 3:25" [Ph.D. Cambridge University, 1999], ch. 1 §1, p. 1; ch. 2 §2, pp. 16–21).

[8] Part of the altar in Ezekiel's imaginary temple (43:14, 20-23) or a feature of the temple in Bethel (Amos 9:1 LXX).

hilastērion itself. The mercy seat was in a forbidden room; only on the Day of Atonement did the high priest enter the room and sprinkle on it the blood of the sin offerings so as to cleanse the impurity caused by the sins of the whole nation. The technical term for the sin offering was *peri hamartias,* and Paul uses precisely this term in Romans 8:3, saying that God sent his Son as a "sin offering" (NIV, NASB, NRSV [marginal reading], preferable to the generalizing "to deal with sin" [NRSV] and "for the sake of sin" [NAB]).

Since this information may be new to the reader, I would summarize these last points: In Romans 3:25 and 8:3 Paul takes two key terms from the Jewish sacrificial cult and applies them to Jesus, saying that Jesus was the *hilastērion* (the mercy seat, the location of the supreme cleansing action in the sacred cultic system) and *peri hamartias* (the kind of sacrifice used to purify the Temple through a sprinkling on the *hilastērion*). So Jesus is being equated with the means by which Israel believed its sin-caused impurity could be cleansed. The implication is that Jesus is the *new* mercy seat or sin offering. But Paul uses yet other sacrificial metaphors.

In 1 Corinthians 5:7 Paul says "our paschal lamb, Christ, has been sacrificed," using *thyō,* the main verb for sacrificing animals. This summons up the image of Christ's blood averting the wrath of God just as lamb's blood on the doorposts averted the Angel of Death, causing it to "pass over" the Jews and seek out the Egyptians. Here sacrifice serves an *apotropaic,* or evil averting, rather than a *purifying* function. Even though the metaphysics underlying the two sacrifices are completely different, both rituals can be appropriated metaphorically because both involve the shedding of blood and both achieve great benefit for the community. Paul is saying that the community benefits from Jesus' shedding of his blood. All that is necessary for a metaphor to be effective is one or two points of vivid and immediately recognizable contact with the thing described. The *blood* of sacrifice connects with the blood of Christ; sacrifices bring some kind of *benefit,* and so does the death of Christ. It may not matter to Paul whether the reader imagines an apotropaic benefit (the wrath of God passing over believers) or a purifying benefit (believers cleansed of sin); the point is *salvation,* and he uses cultic aspects of the Exodus and wilderness story to picture it.

Yom Kippur and Passover were the highest days in the religious calendar and involved the most important sacrifices, so we can see that Paul is making the death of Christ the new, central, ritual symbol. Christ becomes the new place where the community is cleansed or rescued through a sprinkling of blood. Paul wants his readers to see the OT ritual as a *type* (Greek *typos*)—an image that now meets its real fulfillment in

Jesus, the true means by which sin is cleansed. Various typological ways of viewing Scripture were widespread in Paul's time. Paul and other Christians interpreted a variety of cultic events and OT stories as types or prefigurations of the Messiah.

I return to Romans for the fourth area of metaphor I wanted to consider: the social metaphors used to describe the saving *effect* of the death of Christ: reconciliation (5:9-11, 19; 11:15) and adoption (8:15-17, 22-23; 9:4). Reconciliation (*katallagē*) is diplomatic, signifying restoration of a damaged relationship, and can refer either to personal or to political reconciliation. Adoption (*huiothesia*) in the Greco-Roman world usually refers to the ceremonial adoption of an adult, which designates that person as an heir.

Thus there is a change of status for the believer in all of these metaphors. Redemption means a change from slave to freed status or purchase by a new owner. Paul speaks of it as becoming the Lord's slave, which is a liberating experience (1 Cor 7:22; Rom 6:22; Col 3:24). Someone adopted as an heir experiences a tremendous rise in status. Sacrifice means a change from impure to pure status; the sin offering cleansed impurity from the Temple and, by implication, purged the believer's guilt. Justification is a change from accused to acquitted. So one moves from being condemned, alienated, and enslaved to being acquitted, reconciled, and adopted—all of it accomplished by the death of Jesus.

Scapegoat: The Expulsion of Sin

There is a particular usefulness to cultic metaphors: the community is focused on the cultic center on holy days, and Paul would like the new community to focus on the centrality of Christ's sacrifice or his expulsion like that of a scapegoat. Paul uses the scapegoat metaphor several times. In 2 Corinthians 5:21 he says: "For our sake he made him to be sin who knew no sin, so that in him we might become the righteousness of God." Christ is *made sin (hamartian epoiēsen)*, while the community "becomes righteousness." This is an expulsion image[9] with its characteristic reversal of conditions; there is an ailment that is literally banished from the community, and the community takes on the formerly healthy condition of the expulsion victim.

The metaphysics of scapegoating are crudely literal, with a physical loading of sin or disease onto a *body* that is then driven out. This image is particularly powerful for Paul, who is convinced "that nothing good

---

[9] Archibald M. Hunter, *Interpreting Paul's Gospel* (London: SCM, 1954) 31.

dwells within me, that is, in my flesh" (Rom 7:18). Salvation, for Paul, needs to include the expulsion of sin from his *body,* and he finds that this happens through what happened to Christ's body. This informs Romans 6–7 and the early verses of Romans 8. Christ dies "so that the *body* of sin might be destroyed" (Rom 6:6) and "you have died to the law through the *body* of Christ" (7:4). These are confusing images unless one sees the link between *Christ's* body dying and *our* selfish bodily motivation (symbolically) dying. If we are attached to the Messiah, then *our* body of sin is destroyed with the Messiah's destroyed body. Of course, his body never sinned; he had to "take on" sin in a symbolic way. The point is not a strict identity between Christ and the believer but an imagined participation in his death and burial, and then in his resurrection (6:4-5). Paul asks for piety, imagination, and hope—which is not to say that the results are imaginary. In fact, Paul offers no other way to be rescued from the "sinful passions" in one's "members" (7:5). The believer can only be released from the power of sinful sensuality by "dying" to sensuality, and this is done by identifying with the Messiah's death, whereby we "put to death the deeds of the body" (8:13). This is not a careful repair or a gradual reform, but a violent ripping out of sin, possible only because one is joined to the Messiah in whose death and resurrection one can participate.

This is participationist theology. The sensuality-defeating part of it is based on the metaphysics of expulsion, of which the scapegoat is the main Jewish example. When one has been penetrated by the enemy, the enemy must be ejected. Paul is delivered from his "body of death" (7:24) and from "the law of sin that dwells in my members" (7:23) by the dead "body of Christ" (7:4), which seems to be a porter, carrying sin out of this world.

Scapegoating is made to fit within the logic of redemption here: one is transferred to the ownership of a new master "so that you may belong to another" (7:4). From being a slave of sin (6:6, 12, 16; 7:14), Paul becomes "enslaved to God" (6:22; cf. 7:25), living "under grace" (6:14). The change-of-ownership image is linked with the scapegoat image of condemned "flesh" (8:3) and absorbed "curse" (Gal 3:13). This pattern of sin bearing is replicated in the lives of the apostles according to 1 Corinthians 4:13, where Paul uses Gentile expulsion terms when he says he and his fellow apostles "have become like the rubbish (*perikatharmata*) of the world, the dregs (*peripsēma*) of all things," terms often applied to the *pharmakoi* victims of Greek popular religion.[10]

---

[10] Stählin, περίψημα, 84–85, 90–92.

Blending Redemption and Expulsion

The blending of redemption and expulsion is particularly visible in Galatians 3:13: "Christ redeemed us from the curse of the law by becoming a curse[11] for us." Paul is conflating the Deuteronomic legal curse and the Levitical ritual curse expulsion. The "curse of the law" is Deuteronomy's curse against covenant breakers,[12] but the method of repair given by Paul is distinctly Levitical. Deuteronomy offers no *cultic* repair of a *legal* problem. Deuteronomic solutions are not cultic (much less involving any bearing of another's "curse"); they involve repentance and return to the covenant. Deuteronomic solutions are never vicarious: one can only do one's own repenting and returning. The climactic moment in Galatians 3:13 offers a solution that is both cultic and vicarious, so, despite the Deuteronomic buildup, a theme from elsewhere in the canon is being applied. Although explicit language from Leviticus 16 is not used,[13] the dynamics of expulsion are. What Paul describes—a sudden reversal of condition "for us," accompanied by the cursing of some other being—matches the dynamics of the scapegoat rite.

For "redeem" in Galatians 3:13, Paul utilizes *exagorazō*, a verb derived from *agora*, or marketplace,[14] so redemption through purchase is highlighted. The Deuteronomic passages raise the threat of God's cursing covenant breakers, but Paul uses the scapegoat and the purchase-of-freedom images to explain how the death of the Messiah received and eliminated that curse. A few sentences later he uses *exagorazō* again, to speak of the Son "redeeming" those who are under the Law. This would have been a thoroughly understandable metaphor: buying freedom for captives, captives of the Law in this case.

In 1 Corinthians, Paul uses the related marketplace verb *agorazō* two times, in an unmistakably commercial image: "you were bought with a price" (1 Cor 6:20; 7:23). He is making two different points in these two passages—don't debase your body with bad sexual partners, and don't buy into a worldly evaluation of things—but he uses the same commercial metaphor for salvation in both cases. Salvation was accomplished by the Messiah's death.

---

[11] The scapegoat is described as cursed in early Christian (*Barn.* 7:7, 9; Tertullian, *Adv. Marc.* 3.7.7) and Jewish (*m. Yoma* 6:4) works; Stökl Ben Ezra, *Impact of Yom Kippur,* 31, 152–54.

[12] Deut 11:26-28; 27:26; 29:27.

[13] Except for the use of the verb *exapostellō* ("send away") from Lev 16:10, 21 to speak of the sending of the Son in Gal 4:4.

[14] B. Hudson McLean, *The Cursed Christ: Mediterranean Expulsion Rituals and Pauline Soteriology.* JSNTSup 126 (Sheffield: Sheffield Academic Press, 1996) 127.

Since Paul chooses verbs that have recognizable marketplace meanings it is unlikely that *apolytrōsis* in Romans 3:24 is completely devoid
of purchase implications. Having one's freedom purchased by a generous
master was, quite literally, a life saver for many slaves in Greco-Roman
societies. As Bob Dylan once sang, "you gotta serve somebody"; it was
a comforting thought to "become slaves of righteousness" (Rom 6:18).

2.2 The Conflation of Metaphors

If we only observe individual metaphors of Paul we will miss the
importance of his constant conflating (mixing) of metaphors, which implies the blending of their underlying logic. In Romans 5 judicial and
social metaphors dominate, but the sacrificial death still underlies them.
Acquittal in this court comes from an unexpected quarter—not from the
judicial realm at all, but from the cultic realm. It is not the mere *fact* of
his death but the *cultic significance* of the death that produces the
miraculous acquittal. Christ's death yields a *ritually* effective substance—
"his blood" (5:8-9)—and it is the *blood* that averts God's violent wrath:
"now that we have been justified by [or "in" (*en*)] his blood, will we be
saved through him from the wrath of God" (5:9).

Some interpreters who resist the cultic interpretation claim, instead,
that believers are saved by the *heroic* action of Jesus (as in a battle). But
Romans 5 pictures a judicial and cultic, not a martial setting. Besides,
both the Greek and the Jewish literary traditions had for centuries been
interpreting martyrdom with cultic metaphors. In Euripides, Iphigenia
is going to the altar to sacrifice (*thysai*) herself.[15] In 2 Maccabees 7:37 God
literally becomes conciliated (*hileōs genesthai*) by martyrs' deaths. Martyrdom as sacrifice is seen as overwhelmingly effective. Paul takes an
existing development further when he describes the Messiah's death as
potentially reconciling and saving the whole human race.

Three metaphors can even be conflated in one sentence. In Romans
8:3 Paul joins sacrificial, judicial, and scapegoat metaphors: Christ was
sent *in the flesh* as a sin offering[16] (sacrificial) so that God could condemn
sin (judicial) *in the flesh* (scapegoat). The specific focus on "the flesh" at
the beginning and end of the verse suggests a scapegoat image, as does
the idea of one creature taking something on for the whole community.

---

[15] *Iph. aul.* 1398, 1555; from Hadas and McLean, eds., *Ten Plays*, 348, 352.
[16] NIV and NASB get the translation of the technical term *peri hamartias* right, while
NRSV prefers the vague "to deal with sin."

Paul seems to share the popular notion of the Holy as dangerous and approachable only through the correct ritual. Salvation is obtained at that key *ritual* moment when the Messiah is treated as a *peri hamartias*, and sin is *ritually* condemned. It is not "just a metaphor." The saving event comes from the cultic realm, though it acts in the judicial and social realms, acquitting and freeing believers.

The resurrection is usually not mentioned in these passages where sin is condemned. The actual "paying for" or removal of sin is a *transaction* accomplished at the moment of the crucifixion, but the happy aftereffects can be linked to the resurrection.

Paul's system creates some interesting reorientation of different realms of reality. There is a paradoxical penetration of the cultic realm into the judicial and eschatological. Since when is it possible for a judicial verdict to be affected by some ritual action?—but that is exactly what happens here. Further, one is saved by—or *in*—Christ's life (*en tē zōē autou* [Rom 5:10]). Here is a participationist theme: one *partakes* of the Messiah's life and gets new life in court! The sacrificial, judicial, and participationist themes are so blended that a sacrificial death provides vicarious acquittal and opens up access to the Creator's lifegiving power.[17] The end result is diplomatic: reconciliation to God (5:10). The cultic death of the Messiah yields judicial and interpersonal benefits.

Later thinkers have a hard time understanding Paul's highly participationist concept, in which salvation derives from the believer's *connection* with and *replication* of the slain and risen Messiah. How can Christ be simultaneously a heroic martyr, a despised scapegoat, and a vicarious convict? Yet he is, because the bottom line for Paul is not metaphoric consistency but saving outcome. He uses any metaphor that will communicate that, through Christ, we are rescued, reprieved, redeemed. The death of the Messiah had a saving effect; there is consistency in *that*, and in the fact that faith in him means more than belief; it means being *in* Christ (Rom 3:24; 6:11, 23; 8:1-2; 12:5; etc.). Believers must know that they have a connection with the Messiah in order to imagine themselves "discharged from the law" (7:6) through his death. They follow him as sheep follow a shepherd, as clients follow a powerful patron.

Paul is not fastidious about the details of the metaphors and types he uses. Christ is not *just* a sacrifice, and his death is not *only* a redemption payment, nor do the word pictures need to preserve every detail of these

---

[17] Christ *is* the Creator or, at the very least, the Co-creator: 1 Cor 8:6; Col 1:16.

human institutions. The flavor and meaning of each metaphor undergoes change through conflation. When sacrifice is added to redemption, the ransom payment takes on an air of ritual sacredness, while the ritual death takes on the air of a monetary transaction. In Galatians 3:13 the monetary ("redeemed") is blended with the violent sacred ("the curse") and with the legal ("the law")—all of it vicariously achieved ("becoming a curse for us"). The ancient superstition of curse expulsion thus receives a more dignified penal character, while the Law assumes a supernatural character and payment becomes a sacred action.

When one analyzes Paul's soteriological formulas one can speak of "metaphors," but that does not mean that they are purely symbolic for Paul. The "judicial," for instance, refers to the soul literally on trial before God, so it is not just symbolic. It is an event that will really happen. Nevertheless, we see Paul interweaving it with a number of metaphors, so we can study it as another metaphor.

Penal Substitution

Penal substitution is another conflated idea. The crudely literal and highly developed formulation of penal substitution found in Calvin is not in Paul, but a simpler *form* of it is present, I contend. Penal substitution emerges from the combination of a judicial metaphor with some other metaphor for sin removal. In the judicial metaphor a *penalty* is avoided; salvation is pictured as an acquittal in the divine court. The element of *substitution* largely emerges from the redemption metaphor, which is substitutionary in a *monetary*, not *penal* sense.

Redemption can contribute substitutionary meaning whenever it is blended with another image. Blending it with sacrifice brings out the payment implications of sacrifice: the perceived effectiveness of a costly offering. Linking "the redemption that is in Christ Jesus" with his being put forward as a new mercy seat (Rom 3:24-25) means that the redeeming action is also sacrificial and that the sacrificial action is also a *purchase*. This was certainly the understanding of influential shapers of doctrine such as Augustine of Hippo: "innocent blood has blotted out all the sins of the guilty; so great a price paid has redeemed all the captives."[18]

Similarly, scapegoating and martyrdom influence each other. Scapegoating is not literally substitutionary, but transportational (carrying away sin

---

[18] *Enarr. In Ps.* 129, from Eugène Portalie, *A Guide to the Thought of Saint Augustine*, trans. Ralph Bastian (Chicago: Henry Regnery, 1960) 167.

or disease). However, Paul links it with martyrdom, and martyrs were already believed to have persuasive power ("I, like my brothers, give up body and life . . . appealing to God to show mercy soon . . . to bring to an end the wrath of the Almighty that has justly fallen on our whole nation," 2 Macc 7:37-38) and substitutionary power ("make my blood their purification, and take my life in exchange for theirs," 4 *Macc.* 6:29). Thus does martyrdom give persuasive and substitutionary meaning to the scapegoat metaphor.

However, we should not unthinkingly conclude that all instances of "dying for" are examples of penal substitution. There are instances in Greek literature of heroic "dying for one's fellows" in battle that have no penal implications. Examination of the context of Paul's "dying for" passages, however, always shows something more than just the noble-death theme. Romans 4:25 (he "was handed over to death for our trespasses"), for instance, is immediately followed by judicial concepts: "we are justified"; "sin is not reckoned when there is no law"; "trespass brought condemnation" (5:1, 9, 13, 16). Even the question "who will bring any charge against God's elect? It is God who justifies" (8:33) entails a court setting, so that Christ's intercession (8:34) means interceding with the judge. This legal setting tends to confer a penal-substitutionary meaning on nearby phrases such as that God gave up his Son "for all of us" (8:32).

Paul did plant the seeds of penal substitution, although this theme was taken much too crudely and literally by later minds, while his themes of participation, believer transformation, and deification were pushed aside. For many centuries Western Christians have been trained to think in terms of penal substitution, and they tend to impose this concept on all NT soteriological passages. This causes Christians to see penal substitution everywhere, for instance, in Hebrew sacrifice, which they misinterpret as a form of ritualized punishment, downplaying its cleansing and gift-exchange functions.

The beginnings of penal substitution can be found in Paul, but it is very far from being the dominant image. Penal substitutionary theology exaggerates something that really is present in Paul's mix of metaphors.

Multiplicity of Images

If there is so much diversity even within one letter of Paul (and we have left much out), it is no surprise that there has *never been any standard doctrine of atonement*. There is simply too much diversity of conception, from Paul to the Deutero-Paulines to the church fathers and the Reformers. In fact, there *is* no NT "doctrine" of atonement, C. J. den Heyer argues, but only a "multiplicity of images" that "influence one another . . . but also contradict one another."[19] Later theologians try to create airtight doctrines of atonement, but none becomes standard. There is no definitive doctrine in either Catholic or Protestant churches. The idea turns out to be, in fact, many different ideas, but most preachers try to disguise this fact.

What do Christians mean when they say, "Jesus died for your sins"? It can be interpreted many different ways. Did he die as a military hero does, saving his fellows' lives during battle with evil spiritual forces? (That might be the best way to describe his final victory with Peter, winning Peter over from politicized motives and fear of death.) Did he, perhaps, die as a human scapegoat, carrying away all the community's sins? Or did he die as a ritual sacrificial victim, and if so, what does *that* mean?—that he purged the community of impurity, or that he "took on our penalty" (thus transforming "sacrifice" into judicial punishment)?

Did his death *purchase* sinners? Did he *obtain* the church with his blood (Acts 20:28)? If the image of purchase is combined with the judicial image, does it mean that the Divine Judge was bribed? Popular ideas of atonement sometimes assume this dynamic but refrain from admitting it. Atonement ideas always assert a heroic and generous Jesus but usually assume a harsh and judgmental Father.

Actual sacrifice and scapegoating are quite remote from the way we practice religion today, but our *thinking* is still deeply conditioned by our understanding of sacrifice and scapegoat; they stand for appeasement and manipulation, and these psychological patterns remain even when we redefine or spiritualize the religious concepts.

For many years Christians accepted these conflated images without understanding that they were combinations of different metaphors. Some, though, are wondering how literally they are supposed to take the idea of salvation being "purchased," or whether that is only a metaphor that Paul found useful in his preaching. Perhaps it just means that salvation was obtained for humans at some great personal cost by Jesus the Messiah, but any expression of Christ "paying the cost" leads most listeners to conclude that salvation was indeed purchased, that God was paid off. The metaphors of "sacrifice" and "redemption" carry this

---

[19] C. J. den Heyer, *Jesus and the Doctrine of the Atonement: Biblical Notes on a Controversial Topic*, trans. John Bowden (London: SCM, 1998) 130. "No dogmas are formulated in the New Testament"; there is "surprising and confusing variety" (133).

implication. Paul himself argued against the notion that God was manipulated.

Inducement in the Sacrificial Metaphor

That Paul was aware of the crude implications that could be drawn from his metaphors is shown by his attempt to correct any possible misapprehension of God as a heartless judge. After the judicial and sacrificial imagery of Romans 8:1-32, he gives a moving testimony to the certainty of God's loving care, attempting to deny judgmental implications ("Who is to condemn?" 8:34). Paul's intentions exceed his metaphors; that is, his feeling for God's parental love transcends the actual logic of substitution and purchase that informs many of his sayings. Paul is willing to argue against some implications of the images he uses. He wants to show that God was not bribed but acted out of sheer generosity ("God's love has been poured into our hearts . . . grace abounded," Rom 5:5, 20) and free will ("the free gift," 5:15-16). He is arguing against any implication that God was manipulated; rather, "God proves his love for us in that while we still were sinners Christ died for us" (5:8). It was a voluntary act on God's and Christ's part.

Denying the unsettling implications of the atonement metaphors, however, is a daunting task. When redemption and sacrifice are joined, salvation through purchase is strongly implied, and Paul did not succeed in completely removing this implication and replacing it with the intended idea of God's generous and voluntary action. Nor have the best efforts of theologians from the second to the twenty-first centuries succeeded in detaching sacrifice and atonement from manipulation. Denying the heartless judge idea while yet retaining atonement metaphors is still a booming industry, as will be shown in chapter 4, "Defenses of Atonement."

Of course, Paul is not to blame for the primitive belief in a sacrifice-demanding God, which has existed for untold generations, nor for the harsh formulations of people who came after him. However, because of the success of Paul's sacrificial metaphors the fate of the notion of a sacrifice-demanding God is now permanently bound to the question of the interpretation of Paul. His images allow the implications of propitiation and inducement. Besides the Messianic victim as penalty bearer, what Paul emphasizes is Christ as *redeemer* (which also means "new owner," Rom 1:6; 7:4; Gal 3:29), as *pioneer* ("the first fruits of those who have died," 1 Cor 15:20; believers' resurrection is based on Christ's resurrection, Rom 6:5), and as *mediator* (Rom 4:25; 5:1, 9-19; 8:34).

Still, it seems that Paul shares the widespread and largely unconscious assumption that God *requires* ritual, that God can only be reached through ritual. His repeated return to cultic metaphors seems to imply this. It could be that he is using metaphors he knows will resonate with his audiences, but we see him using cultic metaphors even when speaking of his own "priestly service" (Rom 15:16), his "being poured out as a libation" (Phil 2:17), of gifts sent to him as "a fragrant offering" (Phil 4:18), and of Christian life as "a living sacrifice" (Rom 12:1).

The problem is in the metaphors themselves, despite Paul's and others' spiritualizing restatements. The language of *buying* and *offering* and *paying* a price means salvation was not free; it perpetuates the notion of *paying off* the Deity. Paul does not argue that God was induced by a sacrifice, or that Jesus' blood had a magical quality. But those are precisely the implications that sacrifice itself has, and popular Christian teaching has heightened them.

For Paul the real significance of the Temple cult was fulfilled by the Messiah's sacrifice. He raised the *conceptual* value of sacrifice, and much of Christian theology is a reflection on that move. The results are fairly alarming. When believers hear that we will be delivered "from the wrath that is coming," that "by his blood, will we be saved through him from the wrath of God" (1 Thess 1:10; Rom 5:9), they assume this means that God was conciliated or pacified with a payment in blood.

"Sacrifice" implies pacifying God with payment or gift. The long history of the sacrificial cult is a story of manipulation. Either the Deity is manipulated through appeasement, or reality is manipulated by acting on symbols such as the *kapporet*. Much of our religious thinking comes from this premoral level of our religious heritage, and it is still operative within us, though unconsciously. A primitive mentality underlies all sacrificial thinking, such that, even when the believer intends the highest ethical motives and spiritual loyalties, an undertow of superstition causes fear-based manifestations to recur. Fear *is* the underlying psychological motivation in sacrifice: life is unsafe, the Deity is not always favorable; he must be won over.

The most effective religious symbols seem to be, ironically, those that combine new and ethically advanced religious ideas with primitive and cultic ones. The process of spiritualization creates the link, interpreting the old form with new ideas. Under the force of the new idea the cult and its associated theology evolve, but not very far. As soon as the vividness of the new idea fades, theology regresses, dragged down by the unrejected primitive implications embodied in the cult. Spiritualization of cult has a *limited* utility for spiritual progress. It attributes contradictory motives to God. It is as if there were two contradictory instincts: the need to conserve time-honored forms and the need to express higher concepts—a force that pulls us back and another force that presses us forward. The mingling of these two forces causes cult and theology to evolve.

When Paul summarizes his message as "Christ, and him crucified" (1 Cor 2:2), he is appealing to several religious emotions at once. He is moralizing on a violent event, spiritualizing ritual ideas, and philosophizing on Judgment Day. He is able to appeal to primitive levels of religious emotion and to a moralizing and intellectualizing impulse. By mastering the skill of vivid multilevel appeal Paul becomes more "effective" than Jesus; that is, he has more political and organizational effect.

Taking Paul too Literally

Here is another option. Perhaps the only problem is taking Paul's metaphors too literally. He is a preacher, after all, and uses whatever metaphor is most effective at the moment and to the particular audience to which he is writing. One approach to Paul has been to try to deny the presence of atonement altogether,[20] but given the presence of atonement metaphors in all his letters (except Philemon), this is unconvincing. Although the metaphors are brief, they occur at climactic moments in his arguments and are clearly foundational to his soteriology.

Of course, sacrifice is just one of several interconnected themes for Paul, which tends to encourage spiritualized reflection. Other NT authors use the sacrificial image without such blending: Hebrews 9:14, 18, 21-26; 10:12; 1 Peter 1:19; 1 John 1:7; 2:2; 4:10. They seem to be influenced by Paul's formulations, but they lack his conflationary complexity, focusing on one metaphor at a time. Most people want to know: "was it a sacrifice or not? Don't complicate things." Paul's sophisticated and innovative metaphor weaving is harder to follow than are such simplistic formulas as: "the blood of Christ . . . [will] purify our conscience" (Heb 9:14) or "the blood of Jesus his Son cleanses us from all sin" (1 John 1:7). It may have been Paul's intention to say, "keep all these metaphors in mind, because if you settle on just one, and take it too literally, you will be missing the point." And that is exactly what all of the best-known atonement theologians have done.

---

[20] Stanley K. Stowers, *A Rereading of Romans: Justice, Jews, and Gentiles* (New Haven: Yale University Press, 1994) 206–08.

The option I am mentioning here is to keep Paul's metaphors but refuse to take them literally, or to make any one of them all controlling. Christoph Schwöbel takes this approach and ably points out how people departed from the Pauline message when they took one metaphor as dominant and then took it too literally. Schwöbel argues that taking the judicial metaphor too literally resulted in "a rather narrow view of reconciliation."[21] Theologians lost sight of Paul's essential idea that God was not *reconciled*—was not persuaded or manipulated—but was reconciling the world to himself (2 Cor 5:19). God was not acted upon; he was the actor: "Once satisfaction and not reconciliation became the guiding concept, it seemed only natural to see God the Father as the one who received satisfaction from Christ."[22]

Despite Paul's teaching of the once-for-all reconciliation, Schwöbel writes, medieval Christians instinctively felt sinful, corrupt, in a bad spiritual condition, and so they invested hope in the sacrament of Penance as a means "by which the wrath of an unreconciled God can be assuaged."[23]

Perhaps it is wrong to put so much emphasis on Paul's atonement metaphors. Maybe one needs to see them as teaching tools not meant to be taken literally, but as illustrations contrasting the new way with an old way:

- Forgiveness and purification are had through Jesus' death, not through the tedious and expensive Temple cult;
- Freedom is not a story of Israel's past but is available in the present if one is purchased or rescued by the Messiah;
- Justification before God is not a remote possibility but a certainty, if one believes in the Messiah's substitutionary death.

One still must ask why Paul would anchor each of these illustrations in the death of Christ as a transaction that accomplished something unless he believed—literally—those things. Nevertheless, it must be mentioned as an available option that if one learns to take the metaphors less literally one need not blame Paul for the negative implications drawn from his metaphors by later, literal-minded theologians.

---

[21] Christoph Schwöbel, "Reconciliation: From Biblical Observations to Dogmatic Reconstruction," in Colin E. Gunton, ed., *The Theology of Reconciliation* (London: T & T Clark, 2003) 27.

[22] Ibid., 28.

[23] Ibid., 29.

Literal-mindedness can also lead scholars to misunderstand Paul. The real way to assess Paul or any other theologian is to see whether his transformation of traditional beliefs heightens theological clarity, religious experience (personal interaction with God), spirituality (reception of spiritual endowments), and ethics (moral relationships with human beings). Do the teachings speak of the love and goodness of God? Does the prayer life inculcate trust and connection with God? Does the social behavior demonstrate responsibility, fairness, and justice? Then the theological message is helpful. Paul certainly passes the experiential, spiritual, and ethics tests, but on the theology test he gives some troublesome answers, since his metaphors incorporate primitive concepts of God. Again, however, we must consider the option that he was trying to reach the common people and so took popular cultic ideas and transformed them into expressions of permanent loyalty and spiritual progress: "living sacrifice . . . spiritual worship . . . be transformed" (Rom 12:1-2), mentioning nothing (here) about blood sacrifice. Should this not be credited as progress?

It may be unfair to critique Paul's ideas without considering the powerful social factors motivating him to use such metaphors as sacrifice and redemption. These were things that ordinary and poorly educated Gentiles could understand. I can imagine Paul's best efforts to explain the internationalization of the promise to Abraham and the present and future meanings of believer transformation being greeted with baffled looks, and his turning then to the crude but effective metaphors of Christ dying as a sacrifice that removed the wrath of God or as a manumission payment that purchased the freedom of slaves. *Those* images could be understood. They expressed vivid hopes for rescue through the familiar ritual concepts of the expulsion of a community curse, or sacrificial violence having a beneficial effect.

Still, it is a teacher's responsibility to try to lift people out of their ignorance, to explain that evil is not *actually* expelled through violence, that no one is *actually* justified through someone else's blood. Paul goes a short way in explaining that God is not persuaded or manipulated in any way in his antipropitiatory arguments in Romans 5:5-8, 15-19; 8:14-23, but not enough to undo the manipulatory implications of the metaphors he uses. Even some of the briefest of Jesus' teachings accomplish more in this regard, such as his commending the humble prayer of the tax collector over that of the Pharisee who wants to persuade God of his goodness by pointing out, "I fast twice a week; I give a tenth of all my income" (Luke 18:12). What does that matter? God is not impressed. Sincerity is what counts: receiving the kingdom of God as a little child (Luke 18:17). It is the honesty and receptivity of the child, and the enthusiastic desire to hear a story, that Jesus is commending. These are not attitudes that persuade God but conditions that enable the "child" to be receptive to God's grace. Jesus' many positive remarks about children imply the fundamental goodness of human beings, not an inherent evil that deserves endless punishment. God shines on everyone (Matt 5:45) and is happy at the return of any lost sheep or prodigal son (Luke 15:6, 20).

2.3 None of This Was in Jesus

None of this death-centered salvation occurs in the sayings and deeds of Jesus. The gospels indicate that a constant stream of people came to him for spiritual aid, and he extended God's forgiveness, healing, and salvation to them.[24] Without any reference to atonement, redemption, or a substitutionary death, Jesus affirms that goodness comes from good motivation, that people *can* do the will of God, *can* practice mercy, justice, honesty, and trust.[25] He emphasizes God's desire to seek out and save the lost, to give good things to his children, to throw open the doors of the kingdom to those who really want to enter.[26]

These sayings were in all likelihood spoken by the historical Jesus. They meet the main scholarly criteria for historical veracity: multiple attestation (the presence of a saying in several different gospel traditions) and coherence (consistency with the main thrust of Jesus' teaching). Some of them fit the much-maligned criterion of dissimilarity (the likely veracity of sayings that do not fit well with either the Jewish background or with later church theology). Of course, personal viewpoint greatly shapes each scholar's view, and I am no exception. I locate the consistent core of Jesus' teachings in these sayings about the necessity of kindness, honesty, and receptivity; about God responding to human faith and offering salvation freely; about the expansive power of truth (like red wine expanding, mustard plants growing, or yeast penetrating dough); and the setting right that will come in the afterlife.

All four gospels attest that Jesus was more concerned with individuals than with purity codes. He was so bold as to say, "the sabbath was made

---

[24] In Luke alone there are 6:36; 7:9, 47-50; 8:48-50; 13:16; 14:2-5; 18:41. "Daughter, your faith has made you well" (8:48) typifies his conjoined teaching and healing ministry.

[25] Matt 12:33-35; 25:40; Luke 6:45; 8:21; 10:27-28, 37; 11:42; 16:10; 18:17; John 7:38.

[26] Matt 7:7-11; 23:37; Luke 4:18-19; 12:32; 15:7, 31-32; 19:10; John 9:39; 18:37.

for humankind, and not humankind for the sabbath" (Mark 2:27)—
people are more valuable than holy days. He challenged the purity
system and "the whole society created" by it, offering, instead, an "ethos
of compassion."[27]

The teaching that is most prominent in the gospels is the fatherly
friendliness of God. God is "my Father and your Father" (John 20:17).
Really he calls God "Dad," the correct translation of the Aramaic *abba*.[28]
God as Father has at least two meanings: God as the source of our spiritual capacities (regardless of whether we ever develop them) or as our
intimate caretaker and teacher (something we experience only if we
choose to enter into a personal relationship). When we admit God into
our experience, when we hide nothing from him, "Father" becomes a
descriptor of the loving parent in whom we trust every day. "All who
are led by the Spirit of God are children of God" (Rom 8:14). The *fact* of
sonship (our spiritual potentials) means little if we do not activate the
truth of sonship in our personal experience. The individual son (or
daughter, obviously) matters to God and must matter to us: "one must
value the individual infinitely higher than the mass, one must—as
Jesus—be absolutely more concerned with the hundredth sheep than
with the other ninety-nine."[29]

Christianity did retain these values but not always in primary position, and it drifted away from Jesus' own focus on character and trust.
It was not Jesus' stress on honesty, humility, and trusting in the generosity of God that became the heart of the new gospel message, but the
cluster of atonement ideas, grown from the seedbeds of Paul and the
letter to the Hebrews.

In fact, Paul's creative mixture of images was too much for most sub-
sequent writers. The Deutero-Paulines and the Apostolic Fathers take
his metaphors literally, simplifying them and turning them into a literal
description of salvation through redemption-purchase. Still, there was
some diversity of expression during the early centuries of the church.

The cultic practices and social institutions Paul used metaphorically
(sacrifice, scapegoat, manumission, "adoption" of an adult so as to
designate him an heir) have all passed away, but the underlying cultic

---

[27] Marcus J. Borg, *Meeting Jesus Again for the First Time* (San Francisco: HarperSanFrancisco, 1994) 52–55.

[28] Mark 14:36, and preserved as a slogan or address in the church's worship: Rom 8:15;
Gal 4:6.

[29] Eugen Drewermann, given in Matthias Beier, *A Violent God-Image: An Introduction to
the Work of Eugen Drewermann* (New York: Continuum, 2004) 223.

psychology has not. The belief that the gods or God could be appeased or conciliated by a constant display of obeisance and offering was so widespread that it gave rise to sacrificial cults around the world. Though we no longer practice that cult, we seem to accept the common assumption that God is moved by lofty displays of obedience. Thus is God said to grant forgiveness to a human race that he otherwise would be inclined to fry on hot coals for all eternity. The grotesque (and largely postbiblical) doctrine of eternal hell shows the extent to which atonement teachings appeal to fear.[30]

The only atonement teaching anywhere in the gospels occurs in the eucharistic institution passages and in the ransom saying ("give his life a ransom for many," Mark 10:45), absent in the parallel saying in Luke 22:27, which speaks of the Son of Man coming not to be served but to serve—something fully consistent with Jesus' teachings elsewhere—without any self-description as a *ransom*, something completely inconsistent with his teachings. The ransom saying is of doubtful authenticity.

A clear refutation of the idea of the Son being sent to die, and one overlooked by all the scholars I have consulted, is found in the parable of the tenant farmers. There Jesus says the vineyard owner sends his son to the tenants *not* in order to get the son killed, but so that he should "collect some fruit" (Mark 12:2 NIV). In Jesus' teaching, "fruit" stands for good works and other evidences of spiritual progress, so the God figure in this parable is interested in seeing that spiritual progress is being made. He does not send his son to become a scapegoat but to gather together the signs of spiritual progress. The violence of the tenant farmers was a terrible rejection of God's interest in their work, and he decides to give the vineyard to others. Skeptical scholars insist on seeing this as a composition of the church, not of Jesus, concerning God's rejection of Israel, but the church is not known for formulating such elegant

---

[30] The word usually translated "hell," *gehenna*, ought to be translated "judgment." *Gehenna* is the Greek rendering of the Hebrew "valley of Hinnom," where people are said to "burn their children in the fire as burnt offerings to Baal" (Jer 19:5). Jeremiah uses this locale as a symbol for rebellion *and* for the punishment that will follow: it will be renamed "valley of Slaughter"; Judah will be besieged and many will die there (19:6, 9-11; 7:31-32). So *ge-hinnom* or *gehenna* became a symbol for "place of judgment" and was likely used by Jesus, but not necessarily implying the whole scenario of apocalyptic judgment and permanent punishment it meant to some. Mark and Matthew, or their editors, were influenced by the apocalyptic line of thinking. Most Bibles no longer print Mark 9:44, 46, which were added to the manuscript tradition to heighten the apocalyptic judgment content already present in 9:48 ("where their worm never dies, and the fire is never quenched").

stories; Jesus is. Further, the church makes the Son's death the nexus of salvation, but this parable does not.

Another devastating fact is the likelihood that the gospel with the most teaching content (Luke) originally contained not a single hint of atonement. The institution passage in Luke appears to have been altered to conform to the Pauline version of the Eucharist, which was becoming prevalent in the church's liturgical practice in the generation after Luke's composition. There is a huge disagreement among manuscripts of Luke as to the presence or absence, as well as the verse ordering, of the "longer version" of the eucharistic passage, which speaks of his body being "given for you . . . the new covenant in my blood" (22:19b-20). These verses are absent altogether from the oldest manuscript in the "Western" Greek tradition (D) and from the oldest Latin, Syriac, and Bohairic versions but are present in most Greek manuscripts. Even when those verses are present, their location varies in different manuscripts, strongly suggesting editorial insertion rather than scribal error. Westcott's and Hort's argument for the authenticity of the "shorter version," which does not contain those verses at all, is still good.[31] The saving power of "the blood" is not found anywhere else in Luke, and the verses contain substantial non-Lukan vocabulary.[32]

This evidence of an atonement teaching being imported into Luke causes me to question the accuracy of the institution passages in Matthew and Mark as well, though there are no ancient manuscripts to show alternative readings there. But whenever we have a saying that would be offensive to Jewish ears (which any kind of blood drinking, even metaphorical, would have been) and that is found to be a matter of dispute in the manuscript tradition of at least one gospel, we have to question whether Jesus would really have said those things, especially since there is no record elsewhere in the NT of him ever having said anything similar. The Passion predictions do not refer to sacrifice, substitution, cleansing, payment, or even any saving significance to the death, only to the *inevitability* of his being killed after being rejected by the chief priests and the scribes (Mark 8:31; 9:31; 10:33; Matt 20:18-19; Luke 18:32).

---

[31] B. F. Westcott and F. J. A. Hort, *Introduction to the New Testament in the Original Greek with Notes on Selected Readings* (Peabody, MA: Hendrickson, 1988, repr. of the original 1882 edition) Appendix, 63–64.

[32] Bart D. Ehrman, *The Orthodox Corruption of Scripture: The Effect of Early Christological Controversies on the Text of the New Testament* (Oxford: Oxford University Press, 1993) 197–99, 202–09; Jerome Kodell, *Sin, Salvation, and the Spirit* (Collegeville: Liturgical Press, 1979) 222–23.

What an opportunity for him to say something about his atoning death—if he *had* any such concept.

What of the Eucharist?

What, then, did the historical Jesus intend the commemoration event at the Last Supper to mean? It has often been overlooked that the Eucharist could easily be intended as a new covenant ceremony, yet without any appeasing or substitutionary significance.[33] If this is true, then he was intending to build on the covenant sacrifice of Exodus 24:8 but not on the sin offering. A covenant sacrifice is used to seal a treaty or agreement between groups or between a king and a subject group; it was very common in the ancient world. Abraham performs a covenant sacrifice in Genesis 15:8-18. The "blood of the covenant" in Exodus 24:8 occurs within a ceremony of covenant between YHWH and the people of Israel. Covenant blood solemnly seals an agreement; it also marks the formation of a community agreeing to the covenant.

Jesus founded a community composed of those who looked forward to sharing wine with him in the heavenly kingdom. He commemorated his bond with his friends and promised a future meeting. If this understanding is correct, the "blood" image is not expiatory but enacts the community-creating function of a covenant sacrifice. Paul and others give a sacrificial expiatory meaning to the memorial (followed, then, by Mark and Matthew), so that it can connect with their concept of Jesus' death "dealing with sin." Yet dealing with sin is not mentioned in any of the Passion predictions. Rather, Jesus was concerned about his community and the despondency into which they would fall after his killing, and he wanted to give them a promise onto which they could hold. He was telling them something about courage and about the eternal certainty of their community, not about sacrificial purchase.

Another option is rooted in the Jewish Messianic tradition, where the grape cluster can stand for Israel and wine can stand for the Messiah. In the *Didache,* a document dating from around 100 C.E., we see a Eucharist without any hint of sacrifice, atonement, or even the death of Jesus. In the *Didache* the bread symbolizes the bringing together of Christians from many places into one church, and the wine stands for "the vine of David" (9:2), that is, for the royal Messiah. The *Didache* affirms the unity of the church, drawn from many places. Like the previous option, this

---

[33] Thanks to Robert Miller, of Juniata College, for stimulating this line of thought.

one is steeped in Jewish thought, unlike the strangely Gentile-looking ceremony of the church, with its symbolic blood drinking.

Both these options resonate with Jewish tradition, are historically plausible, and are more consistent with Jesus' teachings than is the notion of his agreeing with later theologies of substitutionary atonement. In one of these options the wine is used as a symbol for his death but suggests the formation of a community rather than the bearing of a penalty. In the other the wine is not linked to the death at all but stands for a Davidic Messiah. With these options—whether the cup symbolizes new covenant or Messiah—the ceremony is focusing on the emergence of a new community. The new wine must be poured into some new wineskins, new social forms. What the Eucharist (under almost *any* interpretation) communicates is Jesus' love for his disciples.

The Killing of the Righteous

What did get Jesus killed? In broad outline it was the tragic fact that lazy-minded people always feel threatened by the God-loyal person who insists on asserting values to which they only pay lip service, something observed and dramatized by an author writing not long before Jesus' time:

> Let us lie in wait for the righteous man, because he is inconvenient to us and opposes our actions. . . . He professes to have knowledge of God, and calls himself a child of the Lord. He became to us a reproof of our thoughts; the very sight of him is a burden to us. . . . Let us test him with insult and torture, so that we may find out how gentle he is, and make trial of his forbearance. (Wis 2:12-15, 19)

The killing of Jesus was very much like the killing of other honest men and women throughout time. The crucifixion had nothing to do with paying God or the devil but, rather, with the response of selfish people to one who lives in accordance with truth and threatens to open up a new way of living. Eugen Drewermann writes of the tragic connection between Jesus' life-giving ministry and the death that resulted:

> In closeness to Jesus it happened again and again that people who were crippled for their whole life were able to stand up through their trust in God. . . . In response to his word they learned again to trust their own ears, their own judgment, and their own thinking. . . . People who understood him called him *the life . . . the way . . . the truth. . . .*
>
> Only those who had nothing at all to lose could follow him without fear. All others began at some point to resist his plain truths and to

defend their inhumanities. . . . *Due to fear* everyone has an interest to lie to himself and to "hide" himself, so that he has to kill the one who tells him the truth. . . . Not a single one has the courage to simply be a human being.[34]

As Matthias Beier says: "Not God's will but the dynamics of fear in humans led to Jesus' death. . . . It is Jesus' attitude of truth that is unbearable to a life ruled by fear and the letter of the law."[35] Tragically, there is a "universal mentality that leads to the killing of the one who questions a violent God-image."[36]

I would like to be more specific: Jesus was killed because some religious politicians felt threatened by his independent teaching, his daring to make forgiveness of sins freely available (rather than only through their cult system, which Jesus mostly ignores). The cowardice of supposedly powerful people and the genuine courage of a supposedly powerless man led to a scene of shameful railroading and violence in which the desperation and impotence of violent men was exposed and the spiritual power of the Man was revealed. This was not some cosmic ritual murder required by God. Do not blame God for human cowardice and dishonesty, but realize that violence is the sad result of the tragedy of freedom in the hands of lazy-minded people.

The cruelty of selfish people has no cosmic value; it is not the way of the universe. Even to call it Satanic would be to give it a transcendent basis it does not deserve. What killed Jesus was banal, tiresome, predictable selfishness. People who shut their ears to the truth, who close their eyes to beauty, who slam shut their hearts to goodness, are capable of any cruelty. But let us not blame God for this. Let us stop blaming God for the atrocities we humans commit.

Jesus had to steel his mind to the fate that awaited him, and it was tragically suggestive of the fate suffered by other prophets of Israel before him, so he fatalistically said, "the next day I must be on my way, because it is impossible for a prophet to be killed outside of Jerusalem" (Luke 13:33). He *mourns* the fact that Jerusalem kills her prophets; he had desired to be a spiritual leader, a mother hen, to them, but they would not allow it (Luke 13:34). The rejection was *humanly* determined, and so he had to face the human "necessity" of being killed, just as many others

---

[34] Beier, *Violent God-Image,* 223–25, translating Eugen Drewermann, *Das Markusevangelium, Teil 2, Bilder von Erlösung,* approx. pages 654–57.

[35] Beier, *Violent God-Image,* 226–27.

[36] Drewermann, translated by Beier, *Violent God-Image,* 210.

have had to face death because of the nervous fears of the defenders of religious and political authority. The proof of Jesus' divinity is contained not only in the way he lived his last day but in the way he lived his whole life.

3

After Paul

Paul's theology was seized upon by two irreconcilable branches of interpretation, each of which distorted it to fit its unique viewpoint: the Gnostic branch was drawn by Paul's break with Torah and an implied criticism of all formal religion, and the orthodox branch, seen in the Pastoral epistles, was attracted by Paul's sense of order. The more socially viable option, the orthodox one, triumphed. In the early Deutero-Pauline letters Paul's metaphors are simplified and fused into doctrinal statements. Sacrifice is fused with redemption payment ("redemption through his blood," Eph 1:7), incarnation with ransom ("Christ Jesus, himself human, who gave himself a ransom for all," 1 Tim 2:5-6), martyrdom with redemption and moral repair ("who gave himself for us that he might redeem us from all iniquity," Titus 2:14). The blood *pays* for Christians' salvation: "you were ransomed . . . with the precious blood of Christ, like that of a lamb" (1 Pet 1:18-19). Justification and scapegoating drop out of the picture, and the fused sacrifice-as-redemption image becomes dominant.

There is no longer much flexibility in the use of different cultic, social, and legal ideas. There is only the redemption/ransom, with the mention of "blood" to recall the cultic background. From that time Christians ceased to distinguish among the different metaphors that originally went into atonement. A new, blended metaphor has become dominant, as though all the different images were one notion. Christians now understand sacrifice in terms of ransom payment, and the payment as having *moral* implications (paying for sins), *substitutionary* import (died *for us*), and *relational* significance (reconciling us to God). In Christian atonement thinking they *are* all one notion, one great cosmic exchange. Sacrifice might have disappeared completely into this mix were it not for the theology of the letter to the Hebrews, which focuses on sacrifice.

3.1 Hebrews

Atonement in Hebrews

Sacrificial theology is spelled out at much greater length in Hebrews than in Paul's letters, especially in chapters 9–10. In the description of "the first covenant" and its "earthly sanctuary" (9:1) the author includes a description of the ark of the covenant (9:4), culminating with "the cherubim of glory overshadowing the mercy seat" (9:5), the only time apart from Romans 3:25 that *hilastērion* is mentioned in the NT. He makes a negative contrast between "the priests go[ing] continually into the first tent to carry out their ritual duties" (Heb 9:6) and Christ's "once for all" action, his "single offering" (9:26; 10:14).[1]

The manipulation of blood is essential, both in the old cult and in Christ's replacement offering. The high priest goes into the second tent (the Most Holy Place), "taking the blood that he offers for himself and for the sins committed unintentionally by the people" (9:7), showing the author's knowledge of ritual details. He accepts the priestly principle that "without the shedding of blood there is no forgiveness of sins" (9:22), even though he sees the cult of the old covenant as flawed and limited. Possibly with some unconscious reluctance, he accepts blood ritual as a necessity: "not even (*oude*) the first covenant was inaugurated without blood" (9:18).

Yet the author of Hebrews makes it very clear that the cult's sacrifices "cannot perfect the conscience of the worshiper" (9:9); only "the blood of Christ, who . . . offered himself without blemish to God, [will] purify our conscience from dead works" (9:14). Thus are believers enabled to approach God "with a true heart in full assurance of faith, with our hearts sprinkled clean from an evil conscience" (10:22). Yet even with this clear distinction between the cleansing effects of the new and old offerings, the author attributes some limited efficacy to the old cult, reasoning from lesser to greater: "if the blood of goats and bulls . . . sanctifies those who have been defiled . . . how much more will the blood of Christ . . . purify our conscience" (9:13-14). The new cult supersedes the old, but it seems to operate by the same mechanics. As the priest entered the Most Holy Place with blood, so Christ "entered once for all into the Holy Place . . . with his own blood, thus obtaining eternal redemption (*lytrōsis*)" (9:12). Sacrifice and redemption are closely identified. "A death has

---

[1] This author's style of Greek is more educated and showy than Paul's but, because of the sacrificial theology, the letter was attributed to Paul by some writers, such as Clement of Alexandria. In fact, it is considerably more focused on sacrifice than is Paul's teaching.

occurred that redeems (*eis apolytrōsis*) them from the transgressions under the first covenant" (9:15). Sacrificial cleansing has now been perfected. The new covenant is as sacrificially based as the old covenant, but it accomplishes a perfect cleansing.

Hebrews blends the sin or purification sacrifice with the covenant sacrifice, where Moses reads a scroll to the people, then sprinkles sacrificial blood on it and on them (Exod 24:5-8; Heb 9:19-21). The covenant sacrifice is an oath ceremony, not a purification rite, but Hebrews treats it as purifying (9:22). This kind of typological linkage of Christ with the OT rituals can be called metaphoric, but it goes beyond metaphor. It asserts a real connection, a fulfillment of the old. Hebrews can speak of "the new and living way that he opened for us through the curtain (that is, through his flesh)" (10:20). There was blood, death, ritual, purification, sanctification, and a curtain in the old covenant; each of these also exists in the new.

Hebrews has a sacrificial soteriology, yet there is a mixed message about the sacrificial cult. These sacrifices did not really take away sin (10:4); God does not desire sacrifice (10:5-8, citing some strongly anti-sacrificial psalms); yet Christ died as a sacrifice and we are "sanctified through the offering of the body of Jesus Christ" (9:26; 10:10). Perhaps Hebrews considers sacrifice to have been needed as a regime of instruction, meant to encourage the "awakening consciousness of sin,"[2] but this explanation does not account for the interest in the concepts and details of the sacrificial cult (8:2-7; 9:1-28; 10:1-14, 17-22) or for the equation of salvation with showing "the way into the sanctuary" (9:8), with purification (9:23), and with Jesus' "sacrifice of himself" (9:26).

Besides this sharp distinction between old and new, there is an equally sharp line between earthly and heavenly. We see this in Hebrews' Platonic idealism: the Temple and its worship are "a sketch and shadow of the heavenly," just "sketches of the heavenly things," "a mere copy of the true one" (8:5; 9:23, 24). Christ, "as a high priest of the good things that have come," entered "through the greater and perfect tent (not made with hands)" (9:11), prompting some scholars to think that the actual saving moment was not the death but this entry into the heavenly sanctuary. The earthly temple needed to be purified with animal sacrifice, but "the heavenly things . . . need better sacrifices than these" (9:23). "Christ did not enter a sanctuary made by human hands . . . but he entered into heaven itself" (9:24). Whether the saving moment was at

---

[2] Raymund Schwager, *Jesus in the Drama of Salvation: Toward a Biblical Doctrine of Redemption*, trans. James G. Williams and Paul Haddon (New York: Crossroad, 1999) 183.

that entrance or at the moment of the death on the cross may not be an important distinction. In either case the death is a cultic act with saving and purifying consequences, and it also established a new covenant community. "New covenant" (which can also be rendered "new testament") is mentioned at 8:6-8, 13; 9:15; 12:24. In two places (8:8-12; 10:16) Hebrews bases the new covenant on the covenant written on human hearts pictured in Jeremiah 31:31-34. But the cultic element is stronger for Hebrews than it was for Jeremiah. Hebrews 12:24 says that believers have come "to Jesus, the mediator of a new covenant, and to the sprinkled blood that speaks a better word than the blood of Abel." Innocent blood "speaks" or even "cries out" (Gen 4:10) to heaven, and the Messiah's innocent blood presumably cries louder than any other. Martyrdom soteriology is operative here: belief in the efficacy of a noble martyr's death.

The basic ingredients of sacrificial religion are all still in place, including the implied divine threat, "a fearful prospect of judgment, and a fury of fire" against covenant breakers, those who "profaned the blood of the covenant . . . and outraged the Spirit of grace" (10:27, 29). Although the first covenant is now obsolete (8:13), a potentially violent God is still present, brooding over the process. A punishing God stands as firmly behind the new covenant as behind the old. "God is a consuming fire" (Heb 12:29), just as in Deuteronomy 4:24 and Isaiah 66:15.

Thinking of Hebrews 12:5-11, where the "rebuke," "discipline," and "punishment" dished out by both parents and God are said to generate "respect," "good," and "righteousness," Donald Capps pronounces Hebrews complicit in the ideology of the harsh treatment of children that creates damaged adults, who then think of God as a violent disciplinarian:

> The letter to the Hebrews introduces the logic of sacrifice . . . using it as a theological rationale for the punishment of children, even as it uses the punishment of children to support its view of God as requiring Jesus' death. . . . The sign of God's love [in Hebrews] is not in his mercy, as Jesus taught, but in his chastisements. . . . [W]e become godlike in the degree to which we discipline our own children.[3]

Harsh and authoritarian parenting attitudes go hand in hand (or hand and fist!) with harsh atonement ideas. Capps astutely notes a "lurching"

---

[3] Donald Capps, *The Child's Song: The Religious Abuse of Children* (Louisville: Westminster John Knox, 1995) 68.

prose style in Hebrews, "filled with threatening, even violent imagery," conveying "a pervasive sense of endangerment" and revealing "the profound insecurity of the author."[4] Because Hebrews speaks of God as chastising, Capps is confident that the author was beaten as a child.[5] Whether or not one can know this, one can certainly say that Hebrews perpetuates a stern and disciplining parental model. Yet there are also positive and healing messages in Hebrews. Ironically, powerful religious writing often blends the frightening with the comforting, the time-bound with the prophetic. The simultaneous perpetuation of ancient beliefs and importation of new ones seems to be a common phenomenon in religion. The major religions all involve the continuous, gradual spiritualization of ancient usages. Much religious thought shows a cautious innovativeness yoked to primitivism. Or is this to underrate Hebrews?

Michael Hardin argues that "Hebrews subverts the sacrificial process, albeit under cover of sacrificial language."[6] Abel's blood had cried out for vengeance; "the blood of Jesus speaks a better word, a word of mercy and forgiveness."[7] But I am not convinced; the "better word" is immediately followed by the threat of earthshaking divine retaliation (12:25-29). Hardin thinks that Hebrews' criticism of the sacrificial cult constitutes the rejection of sacrificial violence altogether,[8] but the soteriologic in Hebrews 9–12 is still thoroughly sacrificial. Loren L. Johns's response to Hardin shows that Hebrews uses the language of violent retribution. Despite its spiritualizing agenda, "the letter does not specifically repudiate the violence of the sacrificial system as such even if it has embarked on a theological trajectory that will logically arrive at such a repudiation."[9] It is only in the future, in the reader response to the logic of spiritualization expressed in Hebrews, that rejection of sacrificial thinking emerges as a possibility.

This does seem to be a case where a writer's discourse leads to conclusions that go beyond his own awareness. Hebrews goes so far as to say that the new covenant "has made the first one obsolete" (8:13), and now

---

[4] Ibid., 74–75.

[5] Ibid., 75.

[6] Michael Hardin, "Sacrificial Language in Hebrews: Reappraising René Girard," in Willard M. Swartley, ed., *Violence Renounced: René Girard, Biblical Studies, and Peacemaking* (Telford, PA: Telford, 2000) 103.

[7] Ibid., 111.

[8] Ibid., 113–14.

[9] Loren L. Johns, "'A Better Sacrifice' or 'Better Than Sacrifice'? Response to Hardin's 'Sacrificial Language in Hebrews,'" in *Violence Renounced*, 126.

"the time comes to set things right" (9:10). The new not only fulfills the old; it replaces it. This is a discourse of supersession (replacement). Hebrews is aware of this but does not seem to realize that real supersession, a real "setting things right," would mean going beyond sacrificial thinking altogether.

There may be a social setting behind the concept of Jesus as mediator. Patron-client relations were so fundamental to social relationships in that part of the world that Hebrews thinks of salvation in terms of benefactions provided by a patron. To be more specific, Jesus functions as a "broker," someone who provides a client with access to a high-ranking patron[10] (God, in this case). As mediator, Jesus "is the broker, or mediator (*mesitēs*, 8:6; 9:15; 12:24), who secures favor from God on behalf of those who have committed themselves to Jesus as client dependents."[11] The broker is really a client to the patron above him, and a patron to the clients below him. Through him we can "approach the throne of grace" (4:16), and "grace" is also a term connected with patronage, referring to the patron's attitude of benefaction.[12]

Sacrifice could also be analyzed sociologically, as a form of service by a client meant to earn favor from the powerful one. Even today we speak of worship ceremonies as liturgy (*leitourgia*, service). For Hebrews, Jesus is a better mediator than the priests had been, but he is filling a role they had tried to fill, and so he is pictured (especially in ch. 7) as a priest of a higher order (Melchizedek's).

But to do justice to Hebrews' attitude toward sacrifice and sacrificialism it is necessary to examine it in connection with its incarnational theology.

Incarnation in Hebrews

Since his "children share flesh and blood," Christ took on "the same things," so that he could free them from the overwhelming "fear of death" (2:14-15). To do this "he had to become like his brothers and sisters in every respect" (2:17a). Surprising to many contemporary readers is to hear this last point completed by the assertion that he did this "so that he might be a merciful and faithful high priest . . . to make a sacrifice of atonement for the sins of the people" (2:17b).

---

[10] David A. de Silva, *Despising Shame: Honor Discourse and Community Maintenance in the Epistle to the Hebrews.* SBLDS 152 (Atlanta: Scholars, 1995) 227.

[11] Ibid., 230.

[12] Ibid., 235.

Christ is our brother in experience, able "to sympathize with our weaknesses" because he was "tested as we are" (4:15). For Hebrews, "high priest" means a representative and compassionate figure. His solidarity with the people is the key both to his compassion and to his priestly office: "He is able to deal gently with the ignorant and wayward, since he himself is subject to weakness; and because of this he must offer sacrifice for his own sins" (5:2-3). That last image is purely metaphorical in Jesus' case, since he was "without sin" (4:15). But in his life he really "offered up prayers and supplications . . . he learned obedience through what he suffered," and he was "made perfect" (5:7-9). This offers us an example to be followed. He was "faithful over God's house" (3:6); we, too, must be faithful (3:13) and "become partners of Christ" (3:14). Only with faith can we "go on toward perfection" (6:1 NRSV, KJV) or "maturity" (NASB, RSV, NIV, NAB); both are valid translations of *teleiotēs*. Nor is this an unorthodox or unusual teaching within the NT: "be perfect, therefore, as your heavenly Father is perfect" (Matt 5:48); "God lives in us, and his love is perfected in us" (1 John 4:12); "that we may present everyone mature in Christ" (Col 1:28).

Again we must notice that moral solidarity is what legitimizes the sacerdotal function. The high priest is "chosen from among mortals . . . to offer gifts and sacrifices" (5:1). One of the people, and one *with* the people, the priest can act as their conductor of worship. Yet Christ's is a nonsacrificing order of priesthood, the Melchizedek order. His order does not get its legitimacy through human lineage, as the Levitical order does (7:3, 16). It is God who "designated" Christ "a high priest according to the order of Melchizedek" (5:10) and who said beforehand in the Psalms, "You are my Son, today I have begotten you," and "You are a priest forever, according to the order of Melchizedek" (Heb 5:5-6; Pss 2:7; 110:4). In linking Christ with Melchizedek, the aspects of Melchizedek's priesthood that Hebrews highlights are his nongenetic, independent, superior (7:5-11), supersessionist (7:11-12, 18-20), and "forever" status (7:16-17; Ps 110:4), while adding that Christ's priesthood is "heavenly" (7:26; 8:1).[13]

Christ's character made his prayers effective: "In the days of his flesh, Jesus offered up prayers and supplications, with loud cries and tears, to the one who was able to save him from death, and he was heard because of his reverent submission" (5:7). This is not the kind of sacramental theology in which grace is transmitted regardless of the priest's moral

---

[13] In 6:19-20 and 7:15-16, 26 there may be a hint that Melchizedek's order is heavenly, but by no means is this clear.

character. This is an incarnational theology; the revelation of godly character is central. Jesus' courage, solidarity, and perseverance prove his priestly and messianic legitimacy. The *living of a human life* was key—a whole life, not just the death. In that life the Messiah was tested, as we are; suffered, as we do; learned obedience, as we *rarely* do; and developed great sympathy, as a great priest should. He had to achieve those things here, in a human life. It was because, through experience, he was "made perfect" that "he became the source of eternal salvation for all who obey him" (5:9). The testing, the perfecting, enable the saving.

Hebrews 2–5 contains the most important teaching on the incarnation in the Christian tradition. Especially if we are living in a time of declining belief in the atonement doctrine, we need a heightened understanding of the meanings and values inherent in the incarnation. Christianity must retain a strong christology or it will lose its way. This requires a renewed recognition of the ethical and spiritual values inherent in the incarnation. After all, atonement was so persuasive for so long (and still is, for many people) because of what it communicates about the incarnation of the Word, the entrance of God into human life *as* a particular human.

God is always participating in human life in a purely spiritual way, indwelling each and every human being. But God's participation *as* a human being, subject to all the trials, triumphs, and tribulations that entails, has a unique meaning. In Jesus the Divine became human, finite, and vulnerable, as we are. The term "sacrifice" has been used to speak of the playing out of Jesus' (voluntary) vulnerability. But this metaphor undermines the idea of solidarity between God and Jesus by picturing God as *requiring,* and Jesus as *performing,* a tragically necessary self-immolation. Sacrificial theology tears apart the solidarity between God and Jesus. Sacrifice reinscribes the ancient suspicion of God as chaotic, capricious, and cruel. The notion that God required a human sacrifice is fatal to all tender values.

Hebrews seems to sense this problem. The author stresses that Jesus had to *live the life,* he "learned obedience" (5:8), even though he was never disobedient. He had to be "tested" (2:18; 4:15) through experience, although there was no reason to doubt his loyalty. *Experience* is the key: he "shared the same things" (2:14) his creatures share. He had to take on flesh, or fleshly beings could not be divinized.[14] He is the "reflection of God's glory" (1:3), and yet the culmination of human life. He "created

---

[14] A central insight of such church fathers as Irenaeus and Gregory of Nazianzus.

the worlds" (1:2), yet voluntarily became subject to the world, not for payment's sake, but for experience's sake. He is the "perfecter of faith" (12:2 NAB).[15]

These incarnational insights in Hebrews are yoked to sacrifice, usually stressing sacrifice for purification (9:14), but hinting also at sacrificial payment (9:12, 15). Hebrews seems to have two entirely different, and contradictory, attitudes toward Hebrew sacrifice. The cult was inherently faulty, needing to be constantly repeated (10:1-3), trying to do something that "the blood of bulls" cannot really do (10:4, 11). In a stunning move, Hebrews says that Christ cited an antisacrificial psalm: "when Christ came into the world, he said, 'Sacrifices and offerings you have not desired . . . in burnt offerings and sin offerings you have taken no plea- sure. . . . See, God, I have come to do your will'" (Heb 10:5-7; Ps 40:6-8). Christ "abolishes" the sacrificing "in order to establish" the will-doing (Heb 10:9). The Psalmist is attacking sacrifice itself, seeing it as selfishly motivated, and Hebrews repeats the charge, but in fact Hebrews' critique of sacrifice is strictly relative, not radical. The sacrificial cult is only "abrogat[ed]" because it is "weak and ineffectual" (7:18), not because it is bad theology. For Hebrews, what replaces the sacrificial system is also sacrificial, for, just as the "first covenant was inaugurated with blood" (9:18), so now it was necessary that Christ "appeared . . . at the end of the age to remove sin by the sacrifice of himself" (9:26). He "made puri- fication for sins" (1:3). This is sacrificial salvation: "we have been sancti- fied through the offering of the body of Jesus Christ once for all" (10:10).

These differing views on sacrifice are possible because of the Platonic view that the earthly level is only a shadowy reflection of the heavenly level. Forgiveness through shedding animal blood was appropriate on the earthly level, "but the heavenly things themselves need better sacri- fices than these" (9:22-23)—yet they still need sacrifice. The heavenly temple, too, needed to "be cleansed with sacrifices better than these."[16] The Ancient Near Eastern concept of temple cleansing is here extended to the heavenly level, yet the operative metaphysics is Platonic: the earthly reflects, crudely, what goes on at the heavenly level. "The emphatic use of *autos* here and in the next verse . . . recalls the standard way in

---

[15] NAB and NASB render it correctly; NRSV and NIV insert a pronoun: "perfecter of *our* faith."

[16] Rendering of 9:23b by Harold W. Attridge, *The Epistle to the Hebrews*. Hermeneia (Philadelphia: Fortress Press, 1989) 260.

which Plato refers to the ideal or noetic realm."[17] So temple cleansing reflects the noetic (mental or spiritual) realm. Hebrew ritual is being interpreted with the metaphysics of Plato. This is more than a metaphor, in that the author envisions a real cleansing. The heavenly realities being cleansed are the consciences of believers,[18] mentioned a little earlier as being purified (9:14). In a Platonic worldview human intellects are part of the noetic world, are "heavenly." Harold Attridge notes that Platonizing Jews such as Philo and the author of Hebrews used "language of cosmic transcendence" to speak about "human interiority"; the highest level is also the inward, spiritual level. Christ's "sacrifice has its results in the ideal or spiritual realm where it effects the cleansing of the spiritual reality (conscience) for which the cult of the old covenant could only provide a physical and symbolic cleansing."[19] For Hebrews the sacrificial cult has some limited revelatory value, since it is a shadow of the heavenly level.

Trying to reconceive Hebrew theology from a Platonizing viewpoint leads to contradictory judgments of the sacrificial cult, criticizing it yet preserving the sacrificial concept. The death of Jesus was a "better" (*kreittosin*) sacrifice, but still a sacrifice. The author of Hebrews takes the sacrificial concept more literally than Paul does, even while trying to apply more lofty philosophical ideas to it. He ends by presenting more—and more confusing—sacrificial ideas than Paul does, offering simultaneously a sacrificial soteriology and an argument for the obsolescence of sacrifice.

His attempt to literally reject but typologically affirm the cult is often confusing. Paul does not have the same difficulty because he never goes as far in either direction, never derides the Hebrew cult as weak (as does Heb 7:11, 18) or faulty (Heb 8:7), or gives it a heavenly counterpart. Paul's typology of fulfillment is more biblical than is Hebrews' Platonizing allegory.[20] Paul is more diplomatic about sacrifice, not feeling the need either to reject it or raise it to the heavens, though he will gladly use it and blend it with other metaphors to picture how salvation took place

---

[17] Ibid., 261; he is saying that "heavenly things *themselves*" and "into heaven *itself*" reflect Plato's *Prot.* 360E ("virtue itself"); *Crat.* 411D ("intellection itself"); *Rep.* 438C ("knowledge itself"); 582A ("truth itself"); 612C ("justice itself").

[18] Attridge, *Hebrews*, 262.

[19] Ibid., 263.

[20] This is not meant to deny that there is some Platonist thinking in Paul (some of the flesh-spirit conflict in Rom 6:6–8:13; Gal 5:16-24 sounds Middle Platonist), just that it does not control his understanding.

at the cross. Both authors make use of the cultic notion of cleansing a contagious uncleanness. Neither can say something as radical as: "whatever goes into a person from outside cannot defile. . . . It is what comes out of a person that defiles" (Mark 7:18, 20). Jesus was able to affirm of himself that "something greater than the temple is here" (Matt 12:6)—not a new temple or a new "curtain" (Heb 10:20), but something greater than a temple. If his auditors had understood this, they would not have lodged impurity accusations against him and his followers: "if you had known what this means, 'I desire mercy and not sacrifice,' you would not have condemned the guiltless" (Matt 12:7). The cruelty of Jesus' persecutors derives *from their purity thinking*, which Jesus rejects. Paul and Hebrews, on the other hand, use (and spiritualize) purity thinking. When more literal-minded people inherit the discourse of Paul and Hebrews, a brutal logic of sacrifice follows.

3.2 Ignatius of Antioch

Stimulated by the pressure of his own impending martyrdom, this important bishop of the second century developed some of the most exaggerated martyrdom rhetoric: "I am His wheat, ground fine by lions' teeth to be made purest bread for Christ. . . . How I look forward to the real lions!" (Ign. *Rom.* 4–5); "The pangs of birth are upon me. . . . I am yearning for death with all the passion of a lover" (Ign. *Rom.* 6–7).[21] Of course, this is not just rhetoric, but the preparation for a very real and painful death. Ignatius was bishop in a city that already had a strong Jewish martyrdom tradition, embodied in *4 Maccabees*, the influential but noncanonical story of the gruesome killing of a family of Jewish martyrs in Antioch. "Ignatius does not simply reflect the style of *4 Maccabees* but shares much of its vocabulary,"[22] though, of course, Christianized.

He understands that his martyrdom as the leader of a Christian flock will have a salubrious effect on his sheep: "My life is a humble offering for you" (Ign. *Smyrn.* 10); "I am offering myself . . . as a humble sacrifice on your behalf" (Ign. *Pol.* 2; cf. Ign. *Eph.* 21); he even asks for prayer that "I may be made a sacrifice to God" (Ign. *Rom.* 4), and that his friends do nothing to try to get him off (Ign. *Rom.* 2–4). His death will replicate the

---

[21] From *Early Christian Writings*, revised translation by Andrew Louth (London: Penguin, 1968) 86–87.

[22] Louth, introduction to the Ignatius portion of *Early Christian Writings*, 56.

pattern of Christ's own: "Leave me to imitate the Passion of my God" (Ign. *Rom.* 6). This echoes Paul's idea of an apostle enduring a Christlike pattern of persecution and death.[23]

Ignatius expresses his faith in terms both sacramental and intensely physical: "take a fresh grip on your faith (the very flesh of the Lord) and your love (the lifeblood of Jesus Christ). . . . Through His Passion He calls you, who are parts of His own body, to Himself" (Ign. *Trall.* 8, 11). "For my drink I crave that Blood of His which is love imperishable" (Ign. *Rom.* 7). "There is judgment in store" for anyone, even the "angels in glory . . . if they have no faith in the blood of Christ" (Ign. *Smyrn.* 6).

Atonement is literalized to such a degree that "death," "blood," and "cross" are themselves the source of salvation (Ign. *Trall.* 2; Ign. *Eph.* 1; Ign. *Trall.* 11). Not surprisingly, then, the rituals that encode atonement are taken very literally. The Eucharist is "the medicine of immortality, and the sovereign remedy by which we escape death and live in Jesus Christ" (Ign. *Eph.* 20). "There is . . . but one cup of union with His Blood, and one single altar of sacrifice" (Ign. *Phil.* 4).

Along with this goes a strong affirmation of hierarchy, with the individual bishops next to Christ in authority: "Regard a bishop as the Lord Himself" (Ign. *Eph.* 6). "Obe[y] your bishop, as though he were Jesus Christ" (Ign. *Trall.* 2; cf. Ign. *Smyrn.* 8). Ignatius demonstrates the close connection between strict clerical authority, a literalizing belief in atonement through blood, communication of salvation through sacrament, and anticipation of divine wrath against unbelievers.

3.3 Prominent Atonement Theologians

Greeks such as Irenaeus and Athanasius focused on the saving power of the incarnation as a whole. More crucifixion-centered soteriologies were formed by later western theologians: Augustine, Gregory the Great, Anselm, Luther, and Calvin. The main thing to notice about these five is that they take Paul's metaphors very literally, heightening rather than reducing the implication of an enraged and payment-demanding God.

The fifth-century African bishop Augustine of Hippo is a foundational figure in atonement theology. Augustine seems to see two main functions to Christ's coming. One is to "convert the heart of man," as Eugène Portalie writes; the other is to die, thus "appeasing God"; human sin is

---

[23] 2 Cor 1:5; 4:8-12; Rom 8:17; Gal 6:17; Phil 3:10; Col 1:24.

"an injury of the divine right" for which "satisfaction is due God"; the crucified Christ provides that satisfaction, dying as a substitute for sinful humans.[24] Christ was able to do this because he was "begotten and conceived, then, without any indulgence of carnal lust, and therefore bringing with him no original sin."[25] There is a psychological pattern underlying this atonement theology, a pattern of being beaten into submission as a child, told that it was for his own good, and buying into this mentality of supposedly redemptive beating. "Augustine was severely beaten by his teachers at school," yet concludes, as an adult, that he deserved it because his "love of play" was selfish.[26]

One can clearly see that Augustine is building on Romans 1–8 and 2 Corinthians 4–5, but taking Paul's images very literally. But his claim that "infants are involved in the guilt of the sins not only of the first pair but of their own immediate parents [so] judgment . . . certainly applies to them"[27] simply overlooks other things in the Pauline tradition, such as that "we are God's offspring" (Acts 17:29) and that "the glory of the immortal God" is innate in us (Rom 1:23).

All of the next four authors build on Augustine's notions of a necessary punishment and of Christ as a substitutionary victim. Gregory the Great taught that sin requires sacrificial payment,[28] so that *human* sin necessitated a *human sacrifice*—

> If the victim was to be rational, a man would have to be offered, and if it was to cleanse men of sin, the victim must be a man without sin.[29]

The death of the Son "appeased the indignant Judge."[30] What kind of law and what kind of God is this? Apparently a judge-emperor who can be appeased by the offering of a substitute victim. Here God is understood in terms of Roman law and of an angry emperor who has unlimited powers of retribution. This is the atonement logic that became standard

---

[24] Portalie, *Guide to the Thought of Saint Augustine*, 163–64, restating and quoting Augustine's *Contra Faustum* XIV, 4 and *Enarr. in Ps.* 44, 7, 74, 12, and 129, 31.

[25] *Ench.* 41, from *The Enchiridion on Faith, Hope and Love*, trans. Henry Paolucci (Chicago: Henry Regnery, 1961) 51.

[26] Capps, *Child's Song*, 21–23. Augustine later develops a "view of God as one who scourges" (ibid. 47).

[27] *Ench.* 46, from *Enchiridion on Faith*, 55.

[28] *Moral Teachings from Job* [henceforth *Mor.*] 9.54, from F. Homes Dudden, *Gregory the Great: His Place in History and Thought* (New York: Longmans, Green, 1905) 2:341.

[29] *Mor.* 17.46; Catherine A. Cory and David T. Landry, eds., *The Christian Theological Tradition* (Englewood Cliffs, NJ: Prentice-Hall, 2000) 193.

[30] *Mor.* 9.61; Dudden, *Gregory the Great*, 342.

in Western Christendom, backed up by the authority of this persuasive pope.

For Gregory, "Christ's Incarnation is a sacrifice for man's purification . . . interceding . . . with God as a sacrifice."[31] God's kindness and wrath are often mentioned together; God does always "'blend comforts with terrors.'"[32] God is like "the mother 'who beats her child one moment as if she never loved him,' and the next moment 'loves him as if she had never beaten him.'"[33] This reveals the close linkage between atonement thinking and harsh methods of parenting. Here love is inseparably commingled with out-of-control rage. The pattern is not finished with the work of Christ on the cross. The individual Christian must "expiate his sins," must continually be punished by God to break his resistance; his life, too, "is a sacrifice."[34] This mentality of self-punishment is still imposed on Catholic clergy.[35] Of course, we now know that child beating is only harmful, that it introduces psychological trauma, confusion, and shame.[36]

The next important figure is Anselm, the eleventh-century archbishop of Canterbury, who thought and reasoned within a feudal social system in which "sin" was rebellion against one's lord, doing damage to the lord's "honor." To dishonor one's lord was to undermine his position in society and thus to threaten social peace. Feudal communities were vulnerable; security depended on the loyalty of vassals to their lords and the ability of the local lord (really a vassal to a higher lord) to maintain order on the manor. "In such a community all wrongdoing is an attack on the community. Social status determined severity of punishment," from monetary payment to loss of a hand to the death penalty for the same crime.[37] Often, when the penalty was monetary, a person could provide "satisfaction" through the bearing of some penalty, usually public torture or humiliation. The offending party suffered public *dishonor* in order to restore the honor of the offended party. As Anselm

---

[31] Carole Straw, *Gregory the Great: Perfection in Imperfection*. Transformation of the Classical Heritage 14 (Berkeley: University of California Press, 1988) 173.

[32] Ibid., 186, quoting *Mor.* 33.7.14.

[33] *Homilies on Ezekiel* 1.1.18; from Straw, *Gregory the Great*, 186.

[34] Straw, *Gregory the Great*, 186–87.

[35] Beier, *Violent God-Image*, 283–88.

[36] Alice Miller, *Banished Knowledge: Facing Childhood Injuries* (New York: Doubleday, 1990) 35, 64–65, 130, 135, 171–74; Capps, *Child's Song*, 5, 41, 46–52, 63.

[37] Timothy Gorringe, *God's Just Vengeance: Crime, Violence and the Rhetoric of Salvation*. Cambridge Studies in Ideology and Religion 9 (Cambridge: Cambridge University Press, 1996) 88.

said, "the honor taken away must be repaid."[38] In this system, and in common parlance, "atonement" meant making recompense through punishment.

For Anselm, human sin was rebellion, dishonoring the Lord and threatening the moral order of the universe. Humanity owed God an infinite debt, more than it could pay. Only that particular human being who was also the incarnation of the Divine had sufficient merit to pay that debt. Anselm thinks of a *quantitative* debt of sin, requiring a "quantitative measurement of grace"[39] to make recompense (fundamentally different from Paul, for whom sin is an enslaving power and what is needed is liberation from that power). The mechanism of atonement for Anselm is the mechanism of judicial vengeance in medieval society.

For Anselm, God *had* to require recompense or he would be tolerating disorder in his realm, which would undermine his power. God's honor could not be restored "unless [the sinner] give some recompense for the injury"[40] "or else God subdues him . . . by tormenting him."[41] Manipulation is involved in both of these options, either manipulation of God through a sufficient payoff, or manipulation (coercion) of sinners through torture. Such coercion on the human level would be recognized as corrupt or cruel. Are we to believe it of God? Such crude concepts of justice played themselves out in medieval punishments for centuries. The problem is not Anselm's character or intention, but his failure to transcend the material and penal culture of his day.

Current defenders of Anselm claim that he was really talking about restoring the damaged order of the universe, not God's honor, and they can find a passage where Anselm says that God's honor was not *really* damaged.[42] Still, the logic is that of punitive satisfaction through humiliation, and God is seen to operate by the laws of feudal society. As Timothy Gorringe points out,

> Jesus, following Deuteronomy, insists on the cancelling of debt. . . . Anselm, however, makes God the one who *insists* on debt . . . paid with human blood. The God who rejected sacrifice now demands it. . . . What

---

[38] Anselm, *Cur Deus Homo?* 1.13, from Burnell F. Eckardt, Jr., *Anselm and Luther on the Atonement: Was It "Necessary"?* (San Francisco: Mellen Research University Press, 1992) 177.

[39] Eckardt, *Anselm and Luther,* 112.

[40] Anselm, *Cur Deus Homo?* 1.11 (Prout, 64).

[41] Anselm, *Cur Deus Homo?* 1.14 (Prout, 70).

[42] "No one can honour or dishonour God as He is in Himself" (Anselm, *Cur Deus Homo?* 1.15 [Prout, 73]), right after arguing that "it is necessary that satisfaction or punishment follow every sin."

remains . . . is a mysticism of pain which promises redemption to those who pay in blood.[43]

The concept of justice has (in some quarters) made some advances in the last thousand years, and the notion of an atrocity committed against the Divine Son somehow restoring universal order seems, to say the least, unjust. Anselm's theory offended many theologians in his own time, and before long it was criticized by John of Salisbury,[44] Peter Abelard, and others. The real problem is that Anselm's idea "makes a deal between God and Christ . . . an objective mechanism . . . which enables God to forgive."[45] God does not transcend the mechanism. Anselm replaces Gregory's crude Roman social image with an equally crude feudal image. But advancing human ethics recognize satisfaction through torture as barbaric.

Martin Luther picks up where Anselm leaves off; both "speak in terms of payment of sin, of substitution, and of redemption by the blood."[46] Luther says Christ "mak[es] satisfaction for me and pay[s] what I owe."[47] He retains Anselm's quantitative thinking when he asserts: "The wrath of God against sin . . . could be appeased and a ransom effected in no other way than through the one sacrifice of the Son of God. Only his death and the shedding of his blood could make satisfaction."[48]

That death had sufficient *value* to pay the debt. Luther's formulation is even sadder than Anselm's, since he pictures a divine cruelty that is *worse* than the human cruelty of his time. Luther asserts both the helplessness of humans to break free from the power of sin and the nearly infinite wrath of God against such sinners. Luther recognizes the evident injustice in God tormenting sinners whom he has predestined to be damned but asserts that it is "perverse" to try to evaluate God's justice, that divine doctrine *must* offend human reason.[49] Luther sets up a peculiar struggle of faith wherein the true believer must fight against his reason to affirm what he thinks Scripture is saying. "For Luther the ulti-

---

[43] Gorringe, *God's Just Vengeance,* 102.

[44] Ibid., 101.

[45] Paul Tillich, *A History of Christian Thought from Its Judaic and Hellenistic Origins to Existentialism* (New York: Simon and Schuster, 1967) 172.

[46] Eckardt, *Anselm and Luther,* 191.

[47] Large Catechism II; Eckardt, *Anselm and Luther,* 112.

[48] Eckardt, *Anselm and Luther,* 113, quoting *The Sermons of Martin Luther* (repr. Grand Rapids: Baker, 1988) 7:190–91.

[49] *Bondage of the Will,* 19; from *Martin Luther: Selections From His Writings,* ed. and with an introduction by John Dillenberger (Garden City, NY: Doubleday, 1961) 200.

mate in faith is to believe God merciful when he damns so many and saves so few."[50]

One should challenge Luther on this point. If God's ways are neither comprehensible nor just, why did God give us reason and a sense of justice? Does God expect the theologian to be an anti-intellectual intellectual? Luther sets up an insane conflict between truth and reason, which contributes to the rage he expresses against all his theological conversation partners, whether Scholastic theologians or fellow Reformers like Zwingli or Karlstadt.

Luther finds it "a singular consolation . . . to clothe Christ with our sins, and to wrap him in my sins, thy sins, and the sins of the whole world."[51] This is no metaphor for him. He takes 2 Corinthians 5:21 quite literally when it says Christ was "made . . . sin" when he served as a substitute for those who deserved damnation (all humanity, including children). Thus Christ became contemptible, and the object of divine wrath, when he hung on the cross.[52] Luther *heightens* the violent implications of atonement rather than toning them down as most before him had done. For centuries there had been a spiritualizing attitude toward violent theology, reinterpreting so as to place the emphasis on Christian character and transformation. Thomas Aquinas retained traditional atonement ideas but emphasized human reason and the need to participate in divine love. Luther, however, despised the "Schoolmen" and reviled their emphasis on love and mercy.

That other major figure of the Magisterial Reformation, Jean Calvin, is to be noted for the particular literalness with which he takes the idea of *purchase*: "Christ, by his obedience, truly purchased and merited grace for us with the Father."[53] Calvin's is the most literal substitutionary concept:

> When . . . the mouth of the judge condemns him to die, we see him sustaining the character of an offender and evil-doer . . . [T]he guilt which made us liable to punishment was transferred to the head of the Son of God . . . *our substitute-ransom and propitiation.*[54]

Without such deliverance all people, without exception, would be damned. We are condemnable "by depravity of nature"; all have "become as it were

[50] Eckardt, *Anselm and Luther,* 189.

[51] *Commentary on Galatians* 3.13, from Dillenberger, ed., *Martin Luther,* 137.

[52] *Com. Gal.* 3.13.

[53] Calvin, *Institutes* 2.17.3, in Beveridge, trans., 1:455.

[54] *Institutes* 2.16.5-6, in Beveridge, trans., 1:438–40.

mere corruption. . . . If these are the hereditary properties of the human race, it is vain to look for anything good in our nature."[55]

Luther and Calvin represent a loss of idealism in both senses of the term: a loss of belief in the connectedness of human qualities to transcendental qualities, and a loss in the ability to create service motivation that blends religious and humanistic motives. The Magisterial Reformers emphasize the gap between human propensities and divine qualities, between human longings and God's will. We are told that the individual is utterly depraved and incapable of good—yet nevertheless has the power to test and judge everything, and the responsibility to judge and choose rightly!

This is not to put all blame in the Protestant camp; the Catholic fold had already created a gap between clergy and laity that enabled religious tyranny. But in seeking to liberate Christians from this tyranny the Magisterial Reformers denied any spiritual worth to the people they were seeking to liberate and imposed a new tyranny of self-loathing and anti-humanism. Zwingli began the Protestant persecutions by getting the Zürich magistrates to drown a group of Anabaptists, people who took seriously the call to be guided by Scripture alone. Luther disapproved when he heard of it, but four years later he uttered no protest when the Holy Roman Empire decreed the death sentence for Anabaptists throughout the empire and later signed a decree demanding death for all Anabaptists.[56] Calvin corresponded with the religious dissenter Michael Servetus and then oversaw the process of trying, convicting, and burning him.[57] At the heart of these Reformers' moral failures were two intellectual failures: alliance with the coercive power of the state and attachment to a crude and cruel concept of atonement.

Current defenders of penal substitutionary models repeatedly say things like: "Penal metaphors are important because they take the reality of sin seriously."[58] What is being called "seriousness" ought to be called "literal-mindedness" and, in fact, "a cruel and punishing mentality." Sin and guilt are allowed to set the theological agenda, and the remedy is shaped by primitive concepts of purification and punishment. Jesus'

---

[55] *Institutes* 2.3.2, in Beveridge, trans., 1:250–51.

[56] Roland H. Bainton, *The Travail of Religious Liberty* (New York: Harper & Brothers, 1951) 84–91.

[57] Calvin's co-reformers in Geneva were also complicit in this deed (Bainton, *Travail of Religious Liberty*, 55).

[58] Steve Holmes, "Can Punishment Bring Peace? Penal Substitution Revisited," *SJT* 58 (2005) 122.

concept of God as a loving father is replaced with a stern and judgmental figure who allows a substitute victim.

Substitutionary atonement is based on an abusive mentality, the result of having suffered brutality as a child. Luther's and Calvin's theologies assume an angry parent who is ready to destroy all his children since all are unworthy but arbitrarily decides to show mercy to a chosen few. A loving father, however, focuses not on punishment but on growth. The mature parent is concerned about mistakes, misunderstandings, and immaturity but does not become hysterical about these things. A wise parent knows that a child who receives loving support will gladly co-operate in the effort to overcome these mistakes and to "grow up." Only ignorant parents assume the worst and take out their frustrations on the child, thus creating rebelliousness in the child that they then misinterpret as proof of the child's inherent sinfulness. When the parent expresses rage about every infraction, interpreting every mistake as a sign of dis-obedience, the child becomes frightened and traumatized, and his or her ability to cooperate with the parent's instructions is severely impaired. Parental rage induces panic in the child, especially when the parent's irrationality makes full cooperation impossible.

These are insights that have emerged in the study of child rearing over the last hundred years, and they coincide with, and are *largely the product of*, the values inherent in the gospel of Jesus. The values inherent in the gospel take many generations to emerge; there has to be a culture or a level of society that is ready to receive them. Of course, Luther and Calvin cannot be blamed for living at the time they did. But we should know better now; our advances in ethics and psychology enable us to outgrow the cruelty of the past, although we do not seem to be doing so very quickly.

Besides discussing atonement on intellectual and ethical levels, we need to take a look at the frightening social results on the popular level when atonement is taken literally.

3.4 Atonement and Anti-Semitism

The history of Christian anti-Semitism could fill volumes. Ironically, its height (prior to the twentieth century) was reached during the later Middle Ages, while reason was gaining ground in philosophy, science, and law, not long before the Renaissance. At the University of Paris in the twelfth century Peter Abelard was using Aristotelian logic to examine difficulties in the Bible. This enterprise aroused the opposition of those who considered it impious, including Abelard's saintly attacker, Bernard.

Despite a political victory by Bernard, the attempt to blend intellect with piety became a permanent part of Western theology, reaching its height with Thomas Aquinas, Duns Scotus, and Bonaventure.

Yet this was also the period when, on the popular level, superstition about Jews started to grow. Contrary to much current opinion, the main motivation was not economic envy but superstitious fear of the supposed magical and Satanic powers of Jews, notions related to a crudely literal concept of atonement and of the Eucharist.

The immediate cause for the sudden increase in anti-Semitism is not, at first glance, easy to identify and isolate. There was a certain instability in worldviews and social roles at this time, with increasing social complexity, but we must find more specific causes. One is the sudden increase in Christian militarism in the eleventh century. The inauguration of the First Crusade in 1095, ostensibly intended to take Palestine from the Muslims, also involved numerous attacks on European Jews, with "systematic massacres" in some German cities.[59]

The Ritual Murder Accusation

The ugliest anti-Semitic myth, and one of the most widespread, is the accusation of ritual murder, or blood libel. This asserted that the Jews were kidnapping Christian children and draining their blood for various uses (and here the superstitious imagination runs wild): to heal God-bestowed afflictions from which Jews suffered (copious hemorrhages, children born with their right hands bloodstained, menstruating males).[60] Jews were held to kill or even crucify "Christian children, usually during Passover week, in order to reenact the crucifixion of Jesus and to mock and insult the Christian faith."[61]

The first known Christian accusations of ritual murder leveled against Jews took place in England in 1144 and concerned the fate of a Norwich boy who went missing and was then found murdered. A convert named Theobald claimed that the Jews had murdered the boy in one of their periodic human blood rituals, which they somehow linked to their hopes for returning to their homeland.[62] Theobald had himself been abducted

[59] Léon Poliakov, *The History of Anti-Semitism*, trans. Richard Howard (New York: Vanguard, 1965) 43.

[60] Joshua Trachtenberg, *The Devil and the Jews* (New Haven: Yale University Press, 1943) 50–51.

[61] Ibid., 131.

[62] Colin Holmes, "The Ritual Murder Accusation in Britain," in Alan Dundes, ed., *The Blood Libel Legend: A Casebook in Anti-Semitic Folklore* (Madison: University of Wisconsin Press, 1991) 101.

as a child, forcibly converted to Christianity, and placed in a monastery.[63] Here we see the psychological process known as projection: in alleging that the missing boy had been kidnapped and crucified this monk was really describing his own unhappy fate. In the Norwich case the descriptions of the atrocity were spelled out in highly imaginative detail, but no Jews were punished. That would soon change. Jews were accused and killed in England in the 1180s, in France in the 1170s and 1180s, in Spain in the 1180s, in Germany in the 1190s,[64] and later in Poland in the 1400s,[65] and in Russia.

In another British case, in 1255, a boy, Hugh of Lincoln, was alleged to have been crucified by the Jews; a Jew named Copin was accused of organizing the atrocity. Copin was massacred, another eighteen Jews were hanged without trial, and ninety Jews were imprisoned in London but won their freedom by paying a large fine.[66] There had been a Jewish wedding in the town, and a British writer, Matthew Paris, charged that the Jews fattened the boy, crucified him,[67] "and disemboweled the corpse for . . . magical arts."[68] Thirty-five years later, King Edward expelled the Jews from England.

The ideology of ritual murder was particularly popular in Germany and Austria. The Christian victims are pictured as martyrs who suffered Satanic cruelty:

> The burghers [of Frankfort] painted the "martyrdom" of Simon of Trent on the wall under the arch of . . . the busiest gate of the city . . . depicting the boy Simon nailed down on a board, with bloody wounds inflicted by awls, all over his body.[69]

The Christian response was at least as cruel as the imagined crimes. Politics alone cannot account for such hysteria. There were very strong religious and psychological motivations. One of these factors was increased anxiety about ritual, specifically the Eucharist.

---

[63] Ernest A. Rappaport, "The Ritual Murder Accusation: The Persistence of Doubt and the Repetition Compulsion," in *The Blood Libel Legend*, 306.

[64] Holmes, "Ritual Murder Accusation," 101–02; Rappaport, "Persistence of Doubt," 307.

[65] Rappaport, "Persistence of Doubt," 308.

[66] Holmes, "Ritual Murder Accusation," 102.

[67] Rappaport, "Persistence of Doubt," 307–08.

[68] Trachtenberg, *Devil and the Jews*, 143–44.

[69] R. po-chia Hsia, *The Myth of Ritual Murder* (New Haven: Yale University Press, 1988) 61–62.

Host Mysticism

The rise in anti-Semitism coincides with the rise in anxious attention to the Eucharist, which was often associated in the popular mind with host magic. While this popular obsession with holy and unholy ritual was already taking place, Pope Innocent III called a church council and made a definitive pronouncement on the Eucharist. This was the articulation of the doctrine of transubstantiation at the Fourth Lateran Council in 1215, defining the Eucharist in the most literal terms: "Jesus Christ himself is both priest and sacrifice; and his body and blood are really contained in the sacrament of the altar under the species of bread and wine, the bread being transubstantiated into the body and the wine into the blood by the power of God."[70]

The church's encouragement of worship of the consecrated host was now backed up by a literalizing doctrine of the Eucharist. A widespread *mysticism of the host* characterizes the thirteenth and fourteenth centuries. The poems of the Holy Grail date from this time. Various eucharistic visions occur in these epics. In *The High History*, King Arthur has a vision in which he sees in the sacrament "a man bleeding and thorn-crowned," and the man is then changed into the Christ child.[71] The knight Gawain is allowed into the Grail Castle, where he sees a maiden bearing a lance that drips blood into the Grail (a bowl). Gawain becomes rapturous and has a vision of "a King crowned, nailed upon a rood, and the spear was still fast in his side."[72] In the Grail poems superstition is mingled with idealism, violence with spiritual striving.

Superstition can be creative, elaborating variations on its basic themes. Host magic was one popular variety. People saw miracles in natural phenomena. There is a red bacterium that grows on communion "wafers left for a while in dark places. . . . Corpus Christi Day was instituted by Pope Urban IV to commemorate just such a 'miracle' . . . in 1264."[73] Consecrated hosts became objects of theft and resale to a variety of customers craving special powers: "prostitutes would apply the Eucharist as a sexual device,"[74] and there were suspicions about the ritual usages of reforming movements like the Waldensians. All of this aroused increasing alarm.

---

[70] The decree "On the Catholic Faith," quoted in Charles Williams, *Arthurian Torso* (Oxford: Oxford University Press, 1948) 19.

[71] Williams, *Arthurian Torso*, 75.

[72] Ibid., 78.

[73] Trachtenberg, *Devil and the Jews*, 117.

[74] Hsia, *Myth of Ritual Murder*, 10.

The heightened emphasis upon host desecration which followed immediately upon the acceptance of the dogma of transubstantiation by the Fourth Lateran Council was directed against heretics, whereas the Jews were not seriously burdened by the charge until the end of the century.[75]

Preachers and writers loved to expatiate upon the ingenious tortures to which the Eucharist was subjected—but even more upon the astounding miracles with which it reacted. . . . In 1453 Jews of Breslau are reported to have confessed under torture that they stole the host, as the account naively has it, "to see whether God is really present in it."[76]

Like an idea whose time has come, this myth took root and spread. The presence of Satanic Jews and the need to struggle against them gave meaning to the otherwise losing struggles of the Christian against "the flesh" and against avarice and ambition. Oppressed by shame and guilt, Christians found an outlet through demonization and persecution of "heretics" and Jews. Shame-engendering religious doctrine that offers no way out of self-loathing (except hypocrisy) may drive whole nations crazy, leading them to desperate acts. When unbalanced by fear and superstition people manifest infantile psychological patterns: lies, projection, scapegoating. Jews came to be described as having demonic magical powers: they could cause droughts; they were expert poisoners; they could magically cause dismemberment.[77]

Further, priests during this period increasingly focused on the violence in the Christ drama, and the emotions generated by the crucifixion became more dominant in the minds of Christians. When they looked about and saw the unbelieving Jews still with them, they began to suspect that Jewish hostility to Christ was being acted out in hostility to the Eucharist, in which Christ was physically present.

The constant presentation of the image of the "broken body of Christ," which the believer is commanded to eat, is the underlying cause of the religious madness of the time. A prophet could have seen its origins a thousand years earlier in the ideas of John Chrysostom, bishop of Constantinople, who says that the Jews are "worse than the wild beasts . . . with their own hands they murder their own offspring, to worship the avenging devils."[78] He partially backpedals and says maybe they no

---

[75] Trachtenberg, *Devil and the Jews*, 211.

[76] Ibid., 113–14.

[77] Ibid., 97, 93, 66.

[78] *Adv. Jud.* 1.6, from James Parke, *The Conflict of the Church and Synagogue* (Cleveland and New York: World, 1961) 164.

longer murder their own children, but they murdered the Christ,[79] and so God hates them.[80] Is it a coincidence that Chrysostom is also particularly interested in the blood symbolism of the sacraments?

Fed a doctrine of guilt and punishment, and brought to a ritual that strongly suggested a literal God-cannibalism, Christians became guilty-minded and horrified, and transferred these feelings of disgust to the Jews. Judaism was described in terms of Satanic sacrifice and a new narrative of cosmic battle between good and evil was constructed in which "the tortured Christian children, the bleeding little martyrs, and the abused Eucharist became symbols."[81]

The liturgical reliving of—*participating in*—the crucifixion creates a need to find and accuse some "other" of ritual cannibalism. The ritual murder accusation was a projection of the blood ritual that took place at every Mass. But no amount of other-blaming ever expunges the underlying problem if one continues to believe that God ordained the killing of Christ. God, then, is to blame for the initial ritual murder. It is natural to fear or even loathe such a God, but this loathing has to be kept unconscious, and projection must continue. In unprogressive eras, when the majority of "true believers" are secretly unhappy about their religion, it is very dangerous to be a religious dissenter: "those who kill you will think that by doing so they are offering worship to God" (John 16:2).

One of the terrible ironies is that it was pagans who initially lodged the ritual murder accusation, first against Jews, then against Christians. During the anti-Semitic propaganda of the Hellenistic emperor Antiochus Epiphanes, Jews were accused of sacrificing a Greek in their Temple once a year.[82] Then, during second-century persecutions in France, Christians were accused of cannibalism.[83]

Popes and Reformers

Superstition and xenophobia can be observed in many ancient cultures, but the Passover blood libel is a specifically Christian manifestation. The Jews had become a special category for the Christian. The demonization of the Jews performed a psychological function for ignorant Christians but was opposed by some more educated Christians.

[79] *Adv. Jud.* 6.2-3, in Parke, *Conflict,* 164.
[80] *Adv. Jud.* 5 passim, and 6.1, 3, in Parke, *Conflict,* 165.
[81] Hsia, *Myth of Ritual Murder,* 226.
[82] Trachtenberg, *Devil and the Jews,* 126.
[83] Alan Dundes, "The Ritual Murder or Blood Libel Legend," in *Blood Libel Legend,* 359.

In the twelfth and thirteenth centuries most popes worked against the anti-Jewish pogroms[84] planned by local bishops and monks but with varying degrees of clarity about the issue. Gregory X even decreed that Christians could not appear as witnesses against Jews in these accusations.[85] Innocent III, however, wrote: "Although the Jewish perfidy is in every way worthy of condemnation, nevertheless, because through them the truth of our own faith is proved, they are not to be severely oppressed by the faithful."[86] Apparently *mild* oppression was called for. This echoes the "mild" violence recommended by Luther: don't actually kill them, just burn their synagogues and drive them out of the country. Of course, such subtleties are lost on the louts and bigots who actually carry out persecutions.

Fortunately, there were exceptions to the shameful tale of Christian anti-Semitism. Most notable is the reformer Andreas Osiander, who wrote a point-by-point refutation of the ritual murder accusation. Although his argument was not universally accepted, it ultimately "undermined ritual murder discourse."[87] The Dutch philosopher Hugo Grotius, in 1636, wrote a refutation of the ritual murder accusation and noted that similar charges had been directed at early Christians.[88]

Luther called Jews "the devil's saints" and said their synagogues should be burned and they should be driven out of Christian society.[89] The Nazis reprinted Luther's anti-Semitic writing, using it to support their claim that "decent" German society had always loathed the alien Jew. Luther's polemic is almost beneficent, however, compared with the hysterical fears of the reactionary German Catholic Johann Eck, who perpetuates the blood-guilt libel,[90] claiming that Jews kidnap Christian children and mix their blood in with their matzoh bread. This accusation gives a hint about the psychological underpinnings of anti-Semitism since it speaks of anxiety about the violence and blood magic in the sacrament. A Christian cannot (even to himself) admit to having misgivings about eating the Lord's body and drinking his blood, so anxieties

---

[84] Eleven popes and seventeen theologians are listed by Anatol Safanov ("Blood Accusation," in *The Universal Jewish Encyclopedia* [New York: Universal Jewish Encyclopedia, Inc., 1940] 408).

[85] Trachtenberg, *Devil and the Jews*, 245; Hsia, *Myth of Ritual Murder*, 142.

[86] Trachtenberg, *Devil and the Jews*, 165.

[87] Hsia, *Myth of Ritual Murder*, 143.

[88] Dundes, "Ritual Murder," 359.

[89] Trachtenberg, *Devil and the Jews*, 193, 219.

[90] Ibid., 146.

are projected onto a dissenting religion, and the Jews are accused of having nightmarish sacraments. Medieval superstition was fueled by an unconscious revulsion from morbid Christian doctrine derived from a crudely literal understanding of atonement and of the Eucharist.

Shame Projection

The psychological term for attributing one's own unadmitted feelings to others is *projective inversion*. When the unadmitted feeling is shame and revulsion, the object of projective inversion may be accused of any sort of monstrous act. The secret shame felt by Christians for "eating the Lord's body" is the source of the attribution of blood magic to Jews.[91] Resentment against a God who made salvation dependent on a ritual murder and demanded that it be relived in liturgy motivates the myth of Jewish ritual murder of Christian children. (The principal symbol of Christ in those days was the Christ *child*). Christians dealt with their anxiety and resentment by projecting their shame feelings onto the Jews.

European anti-Semitism is, at bottom, anti-Christianity. The irony is that many Jews nowadays are nonreligious, but Jews still *symbolize* religion for Christians; they stand for the whole biblical story. If one is uncomfortable with that story, one can always kill the messenger, either claiming that there is no truth in the message (as the Nazis and Soviets did), or claiming to embrace its truth (while actually betraying Jesus' message about honesty, faith, and responsibility).

The explosive rage Christians have often directed against their parental religion is really rage at the impossible binds to which distorted Christian teaching has brought them. Projective inversion is an irresponsible way of dealing with the inner shame created by errant teaching. Muslim anti-Semitism (anti-Israeli bias, if you like) functions the same way: secret frustration with the shaming and cruelty in one's own religion finds an outlet by demonizing the Jewish religion. Every anti-Semite is secretly an anti-Christian or an anti-Muslim. "And they will do this because they have not known the Father or me" (John 16:3). No one who really knows Jesus can be an anti-Semite.

Concepts of a violent and sacrifice-demanding God lead to pathological human results. A bad tree produces bad fruit. The bad tree is imagining a cruel God who gives contradictory instructions and so is always liable to break out in anger. This God concept generates fear, but Jesus

---

[91] Dundes, "Ritual Murder," 344, 352–55.

put trust in place of fear—"fear not" and "be of good cheer"[92] were more or less the slogans of his ministry—and he taught that the "little ones" are precious in God's sight.[93]

---

[92] Rendered "take heart" or "take courage" in NRSV.
[93] Matt 9:2; 14:27; 18:14; Luke 5:10; 12:24, 32; John 10:28; 14:27; 16:33; 21:15.

4

Defenses of Atonement

I would now consider the options on atonement taken by various scholars. In so doing I have found it convenient to divide them between those giving "defenses of atonement" and those providing "critiques of atonement," although in fact some theories of atonement are criticized by the "defenders" and other theories are promoted by various "critics." Still, this division allows for a helpful progression through the various options.

I start with some observations about sacrifice. Ancient sacrifice was motivated to "find favor in your sight," to use the common OT expression.[1] Atonement doctrine reshapes the ancient sentiment, "May he remember all your offerings, and regard with favor your burnt sacrifices" (Ps 20:3). Paul the preacher used metaphors that carried implications of inducement, although Paul the theologian never defended those implications. Paul was, however, first and foremost a preacher who was willing to go to great lengths to reach his audience. His successes carried a theological cost that we are now paying. It has become clear that Paul yoked together contradictory ideas of God: some are securely based in the parental love of God, others revert to manipulative cultic concepts. An intense religious experience (both for Paul and for the early church) prevented this contradiction from becoming a problem at first, but the problem emerged with a vengeance in the Middle Ages and now can hardly be avoided. Continued rationalizing of atonement by many writers and preachers serves to disguise the problem and avoid the issue.

Most theologians claim to accept the prophetic principle that God cannot be persuaded through sacrificial offerings, yet that is just what

[1] Exod 33:16; 34:9; Lev 26:9, 45; Deut 33:16; Judg 6:17; Pss 85:1; 119:58.

is implied in all doctrines of intercessory atonement. What are the consequences of believing in the aversion of divine retribution by a ritual payment? Does it not assume a stern and unfeeling God who yet can be bribed? This is a troubling image! What kind of judge requires punishment but is content to allow the punishment of the innocent? Do we accept this idea, reject it, get a more accurate explanation, create a spiritualizing explanation that denies its violence, or declare it to be true even though we cannot fathom it? What are our options?

Many current defenders of these doctrines seem to not recognize the violence and manipulation implicit in the metaphors. Others use a spiritualizing strategy, upholding the higher intentions of biblical authors while downplaying the primitive elements. Only a few reject the discourse of sacrifice and scapegoat as primitive legacies hindering our understanding of the gospel. Some argue that God is genuinely parental, not demanding an impossible purity or a magical restoration of innocence but only wanting the *maturation* of the children (as a good parent does).

Colin Gunton tries to downplay the violent origins of atonement; Hans Boersma says God *has* to be violent when acting in a violent human environment; René Girard says God rejects violence but made use of the violent death of Jesus in order to expose violence; Jack Nelson-Pallmeyer says God never uses violence. This is just a sampling of the options to be considered in the A sections below. In the B sections I summarize my misgivings about these approaches and suggest some solutions, moving toward the expression of a philosophical position.

4.1A Orthodox Defenses

Schmiechen's Ten Theories of Atonement

Among books in defense of atonement, Peter Schmiechen's *Saving Power* is the best recent effort in terms of extensiveness and incisiveness. This is not only because of his ability to make distinctions—he discerns *ten* different theories of atonement[2]—but also because of his clearheaded rejection of some of the crude, but popular, theories.

In discussing the first concept of atonement (sacrifice), Schmiechen focuses on the letter to the Hebrews. He notes that atonement there is

---

[2] These are sacrifice, justification, penal substitution, liberation, renewal of creation, restoration of creation, Christ the goal of creation, Christ the way to knowledge of God, Christ the reconciler, and the love of God (Peter Schmiechen, *Saving Power: Theories of Atonement and Forms of the Church* [Grand Rapids: Eerdmans, 2005] vii–viii).

"paradoxical. The conclusion moves in two opposing directions . . . Jesus fulfills the requirements of priestly sacrifice . . . Jesus so surpasses the Levitical system that sacrifice is actually abolished."[3] Schmiechen has no serious problems with Hebrews since, he argues, it does not speak of God being paid off. He is able to convince himself (errantly, I believe) that "Hebrews stays clearly within the tradition of sin offering for purification,"[4] that the sacrificial idea being argued in passages like Hebrews 9:23 is simply impurity-purgation. But sacrifice means more than that for Hebrews; it also "obtain[s] eternal redemption . . . a death . . . that redeems" (9:12, 15); sacrificial blood establishes a covenant, brings about forgiveness, makes intercession with God (9:18, 22; 7:25). Consciences are purified and believers are sanctified through "the blood" (9:14; 13:12) or "the body" (10:10). Schmiechen does not wish to confront the violent and primitive sacrificial thinking in Hebrews, where the only options are obtaining "a sacrifice for sins" or suffering "a fearful prospect of judgment, and a fury of fire" (10:26-27).

Schmiechen's survey of Luther is competent, though he gives only a few instances of Luther's tendency toward immoderate rhetoric, his calling the Scholastics "pig theologians," for instance.[5] He does show that "Luther totally rejects the idea of ordered love" and of human effort toward loving God; instead, "the self is caught up in a closed world of selfishness and enmity against God."[6]

Schmiechen critiques the Calvinist theory of penal substitution for being based on notions of "retributive atonement,"[7] because it "makes God passive as well as vengeful," makes the death of Christ something "required by retributive justice,"[8] and has God "demanding satisfaction prior to any act of forgiveness."[9] Nor is it any solution to exercise the "trinitarian defense," which "simply transfers the problem to the internal life of God," with the Son offering satisfaction to the Father; there is always a problem when theologians try to build on "the heavy-laden words *appease, earn, and propitiate.*"[10]

---

[3] Schmiechen, *Saving Power*, 34.

[4] Ibid., 36.

[5] "It is sheer madness to say that man can love God above everything by his own powers. . . . O you fools, you pig-theologians!" (from *Lectures on Romans* [Philadelphia: Westminster, 1961] 129), quoted in Schmiechen, *Saving Power*, 68 n. 24.

[6] Schmiechen, *Saving Power*, 69.

[7] Ibid., 38.

[8] Ibid., 40.

[9] Ibid., 195.

[10] Ibid., 40–41.

He notes that the Catholic tradition has sometimes changed its emphasis, usually "by adding to the tradition, rather than subtracting from the tradition."[11] The *Catechism of the Catholic Church*, published in 1995, pushes retributive justice "to the background," instead emphasizing Christ as Incarnate Word who teaches love and obedience and whose "death brings liberation from sin."[12] He notes that Aquinas had already attempted this "shift from the death of Jesus as the cause of salvation to Jesus' obedience" [as the cause of salvation].[13] Schmiechen acknowledges that it is "troublesome" to have a theology where "death per se is the active cause of salvation."[14]

Schmiechen prefers to attack not Calvin, but the Calvinist penal substitutionary model expressed by the nineteenth-century author Charles Hodge. Penal substitution is fatally flawed because "We end up with the domination of a particular kind of justice over the entire theological agenda"; it "requires the Law to remain in full force," and its implacable emphasis on penalty means "it degenerates into vengeance."[15] The stress on punishment and substitution "is quite contrary to the evangelical message of the New Testament," nor is there any relief by picturing it as a transaction within the Trinity: "Does justice only belong to the Father and love only belong to the Son?"[16]

Schmiechen's defense of Anselm is interesting but not convincing. He argues that it is not honor as "moral sovereignty" that prompts God to send his Son, but "honor as covenant faithfulness" (love, in other words). Anselm provides an allegory of someone finding a pearl in the mud and cleaning it up (I, 19) and remarks, in Schmiechen's words, "so God shall take up what has been defiled and restore it."[17] Thus Anselm never says that Jesus' "life was demanded by God to comply with penal justice. His death was a gift that he offered to God."[18] Thus does Schmiechen almost make one forget that "satisfaction" is medieval language for restitution through suffering, entirely based in the legal system, and not a "gift" (vengeance as a gift?). Schmiechen is at his least convincing in this chapter.

---

[11] Ibid., 49–50.
[12] Ibid., 49.
[13] Ibid., 52.
[14] Ibid., 72.
[15] Ibid., 110–11.
[16] Ibid., 112.
[17] Ibid., 206.
[18] Ibid., 216.

The most original suggestion comes in Schmiechen's stunning tenth chapter, which discovers another theory of atonement in Paul, completely unrelated to the sacrificial image. This is the model of "Christ the Reconciler." Jesus shows us how to overcome our constant hostility, party factionalism, and violence. In this model Christ "*overcomes* the violence of the world by refusing to respond in kind. By his resistance he breaks the cycle of violence."[19] This is an ethical interpretation, focused on overcoming "the alienation between warring factions."[20] Into the maelstrom of human hostility, God steps:

> God suffers the hostility . . . that the world might see what it has become. . . . Jesus dies the death reserved for sinners, which is always the case of the innocent. . . . He did this for our sake, not as an offering to God. Its purpose was that in him we might be . . . at peace with one another and with God.[21]

This resembles what is said by a number of other ethical interpreters, from Abelard to the Mennonites. It places the stress on what we are meant to learn: "a willingness to set aside one's claims and join Christ in resisting and overcoming the ways of the world with saving power."[22] I would like to see this approach blended with the recent advances in family ethics, where people have come to realize how deeply ingrained and harmful is the practice of beating children, something that is handed down from generation to generation and that requires someone to *break the cycle of violence.* On the public level Christ did break the cycle of violence, and in his teachings he gives us abundant basis for more enlightened treatment of children. In fact, Jesus makes childlike honesty an essential for entering the kingdom, admonishes the leaders in his movement to allow children to come to him (Mark 10:14-16; Matt 18:1-10), and (most importantly for reviving a concept of the goodness of God) links his attitude to God's: "whatever the Father does, the Son does likewise" (John 5:19). These insights could add considerable value to the understanding of "Christ the Reconciler," something Schmiechen finds in 1 Corinthians 1–2, but that I find throughout the gospels and Paul— although I do not call it "atonement," as that word suggests sacrifice, scapegoating, and satisfaction.

---

[19] Ibid., 282.
[20] Ibid., 279.
[21] Ibid., 284.
[22] Ibid., 287.

One way to divert attention from the more barbaric atonement concepts is to direct attention to more advanced teachings and call them "atonement." Some English-language authors have found this task easy to perform, since the English word "atonement" does not derive from sacrificial terminology but comes from the combination "at-one-ment," meaning reconciliation with God or unity with God's will: "unity . . . as the center of atonement."[23] Of course, Schmiechen is writing in German, yet he moves in the same direction with his option number ten. It needs to be stressed, however, that this option is incompatible with the sacrificial and penal options, which see Jesus *having* to die to satisfy some implacable law before God could extend forgiveness.

Coming from a very different (Heideggerian) viewpoint, David Odell-Scott comes up with a formula remarkably similar to Schmiechen's tenth option. Building on the etymology of the English word at-one-ment, Odell-Scott emphasizes reconciliation and reunification. Thus he can translate 2 Corinthians 5:19, "God was re-calling the world to himself," or "God was at-oning the world to himself."[24] He notes that this "does not occur *in the world*. The reconciling of the world to God occurs 'in Christ.'"[25] "The atoning 'in Christos' is the at-oning of differences."[26] Aside from these useful observations, however, his approach wallows in nihilistic variations on Heideggerian themes: Christ turns out to be "a nonidentity or difference which overcomes itself in the play of the difference of identity and the identity of difference."[27] This is *not different enough* from Heidegger and Derrida.

Rahner and Balthasar

An interesting debate takes place between two men who may have been the leading Roman Catholic theologians of the twentieth century. Karl Rahner is the one who is more receptive to scientific and historical-critical viewpoints, while Hans Urs von Balthasar is eager to defend orthodoxy against all comers, including those who give an inadequate

[23] Patricia A. Williams, *Doing without Adam and Eve: Sociobiology and Original Sin.* Theology and the Sciences (Minneapolis: Fortress Press, 2001) 181. See also "atonement as revelation" (Abelard) and "atonement as transformation" (Athanasius) (195–96). But these have nothing to do with cultic atonement or satisfaction.

[24] David W. Odell-Scott, *A Post-Patriarchal Christology.* AARA 78 (Atlanta: Scholars Press, 1991) 229.

[25] Ibid., 230.

[26] Ibid., 231.

[27] Ibid., 236.

retelling of the divine drama. Rahner is taking more intellectual risks and consequently must be more cautious in his delivery; Balthasar can come across as more bold because he takes fewer risks. Balthasar unabashedly defends the *sacrum commercium*, "the price paid,"[28] "the union of God and human through the 'exchange of places,'"[29] and finds Rahner inadequate in this connection: "Like all systems that fail to take the *sacrum commercium* seriously, Rahner's soteriology lacks the decisive dramatic element. Thus God's 'wrath' is always, antecedently, overtaken by his will to save."[30]

Thus, according to Balthasar, Rahner is guilty of focusing on God's constant motivation to save, leaving the threat of damnation out of the concrete "drama" played out in the Passion of Christ. Balthasar rejects Rahner's approach, saying it is not correct to "take references to God's anger" and simply "dissolve them in 'God's free, salvific will,'"[31] although what Rahner actually says is, "God's free, salvific will [is] the *a priori* cause of the Incarnation and of the cross of Christ, a cause which is not conditional upon anything outside God."[32] In other words, God is not forced (by sin) to resort to the incarnation. Balthasar is not comfortable with the implications of this. In fact, he is quite scandalized by Rahner, for instance by his effort to "return to the original revelation" coming from Jesus himself, who may not even have regarded his coming death as having "redemptive significance."[33] Indeed, Rahner does say something that is now becoming accepted by more and more scholars: "it is not established historically beyond dispute whether the pre-resurrection Jesus . . . interpreted his death as an expiatory sacrifice."[34]

Balthasar defends traditional atonement formulas, insisting that "redemption from the powers hostile to God must be 'paid for.'"[35] He commends Anselm's satisfaction theory. He has no problem with "*Satisfactio* . . . a 'ransom,' *redemptio* . . . paid for by a 'price,' *pretium*,"[36] but he rejects the idea of "a cruel Father-God . . . demand[ing] that this Son

[28] Hans Urs von Balthasar, *Theo-Drama: Theological Dramatical Theory*. Vol. 4: *The Action* (San Francisco: Ignatius Press, 1994) 249.

[29] Ibid., 266.

[30] Ibid., 283.

[31] Ibid., 275.

[32] Karl Rahner, *Foundations of Christian Faith: An Introduction to the Idea of Christianity*, trans. William Dych (New York: Seabury, 1978) 317.

[33] Balthasar, *Theo-Drama* 4:274, referring to Rahner, *Foundations*, 265–66 and 282–83.

[34] Rahner, *Foundations*, 283.

[35] Balthasar, *Theo-Drama* 4:245.

[36] Ibid., 260, citing *Cur deus homo* 1.1.3 and 6; 2.16, 20–21.

should be slaughtered" and defends Anselm against the accusation that his theology promulgates such an idea.[37] He does, however, criticize Anselm for failing to "see that Jesus' entire life, work and suffering are meritorious," and that the incarnation establishes an "organic connection between Christ and all other human beings."[38] Saying that Anselm's idea is insufficiently incarnational is, in fact, saying that it is too *transactional*. But Balthasar never considers the possibility that transactional concepts are inherently problematic because they imply that God was *persuaded* by what took place at the crucifixion. He does not have a problem with Augustine's and Anselm's notions of the crucifixion as a transaction with God.

Rahner takes much more seriously than Balthasar the fact of "God's sovereign immutability, because he cannot be influenced or moved."[39] Naturally, then, he has difficulty with doctrines that have God's wrath being assuaged or God repenting of his intentions. Rahner does not want "redemption . . . misunderstood in a mythological way as causing some change of mind on God's part."[40] Balthasar resents Rahner's raising the issue at all,[41] but it is one that needed to be raised if he was going to say things to which thoughtful and educated people would listen. "The idea of propitiating the divinity by means of a sacrifice was a current notion" that was utilized in the NT, but it "offers little help to us today" and it contradicts the principle "that God's mind cannot be 'changed' . . . (and the New Testament is aware of this too)."[42] If one asserts that God "loves the sinner originally and without reasons" one has already criticized "the notion of an expiatory sacrifice."[43]

Wheeler: Expanding Atonement

David Wheeler has written a well-organized book that links biblical with process theology, draws on objective and subjective theories of atonement, and promotes atonement from a onetime event to a continuing process in the human race, thus identifying atonement with all spiritual progress: "We progressively become in our life process what we are

[37] Balthasar, *Theo-Drama* 4:259 n. 12.
[38] Ibid., 261.
[39] Rahner, *Foundations*, 317.
[40] Ibid., 211.
[41] Balthasar, *Theo-Drama* 4:275.
[42] Rahner, *Foundations*, 282.
[43] Ibid., 283.

declared to be by God. . . . [O]ne's realization of 'atonedness' is partial and imperfect until the end of the age."[44] "Atonement is consummated through and only through the real response of free human agents."[45]

Wheeler is redefining atonement as "reordering of broken or distorted relationship," which involves a change in humanity but also some change in "our hybrid God"[46] (a God both immanent and transcendent). This is a concept from process theology, in which God emerges in the world process: "God is responsive and vulnerable to the world, but not totally dependent upon it for his actualization."[47]

Wheeler's concept itself is hybrid, finding no real contradiction between propitiatory sin-bearing or ransom-paying and "the 'simple' Jesus sayings."[48] This glosses over real differences. Further, he spiritualizes sacrifice; that is, he pours spiritual meanings into old ritual wineskins, downplaying the violent thinking in the ritual: "*Sacrifice* presents us, when properly understood, not with a transaction, but a self-dedication symbolically accomplished, a self-surrender of the convicted sinner to his or her God. Atonement is at its root relational."[49]

Wheeler commends Schleiermacher's and Teilhard de Chardin's affirmation of a continuity between God's redeeming activity and his creative activity.[50] Christ's emergence *within* history also bespeaks a continuity between "nature and grace."[51] Human struggle and Christ's leadership (Teilhard's idea of Christ as the overseer of evolution) go together, though Wheeler can also criticize a certain determinism in Teilhard.[52]

In the end Wheeler's is a worthy project, but incomplete. Since he glosses over most difficulties it is hard to know exactly how he would synthesize Teilhard with Rahner, Barth with Schleiermacher.

Gunton: A Non-Denial Denial of Penal Substitution

A fairly common strategy is to use the logic of substitutionary punishment and payoff while boldly denying that this is being done. Colin

---

[44] David L. Wheeler, *A Relational View of the Atonement: Prolegomenon to a Reconstruction of the Doctrine.* American University Studies, Series 7, Theology and Religion 54 (New York: Peter Lang, 1989) 223.

[45] Ibid., 182.

[46] Ibid., 190.

[47] Ibid., 84.

[48] Ibid., 154–55.

[49] Ibid., 113.

[50] Ibid., 116, 176.

[51] Ibid., 186.

[52] Ibid., 180–82, 227.

Gunton is one of the better-known examples of this approach. First he must deny that biblical sacrifice has any of the motives that characterize nonbiblical sacrifice. He allows that

> In most sacrificial systems, sacrifice is something people give to God: in some of them as a means by which the deity is appeased or "bought off"; in the Bible more as a gift to the God who by virtue of who he is cannot be bought. When Christ is described as a sacrifice, the notion of gift remains, but . . . the primary giver is God.[53]

This evades the fact that the common people of Israel *did* conceive of sacrifice as appeasing or buying off and that this was precisely the concept that was vigorously attacked by prophets[54] and psalmists[55] who saw sacrifice as a false solution for sins, some of them even attacking the whole priestly system: "I did not speak to [your ancestors] or command them concerning burnt offerings and sacrifices" (Jer 7:22; cf. Amos 5:23-25); "Sacrifice and offering you do not desire" (Ps 40:6); "because you have rejected knowledge, I reject you from being a priest to me. . . . For I desire steadfast love and not sacrifice" (Hos 4:6; 6:6).

Elsewhere Gunton defends the "primitive" saying that sacrifice has to do with "the ordering and reordering of life," with "the rightful ordering of life in the world."[56] He whitewashes sacrifice to make it an inoffensive metaphor. He makes sacrifice mean much more than it meant to its practitioners: "May it not be that we encounter not 'mere' metaphors but linguistic usages which demand a new way of thinking about and living in the world? Here is *real* sacrifice, victory and justice, so that what we thought the words meant is shown to be inadequate."[57]

This is a spiritualizing or moralizing strategy, importing moral meanings from other realms and applying them to the cult.[58] This enables Gunton to modernize "sacrifice," to suppress its commercial and selfish side. By this I do not mean a selfishness in Jesus or God, but the selfishness of the sacrificial mentality itself, which thinks to persuade God with a display of giving or of suffering. An example of this mentality is evident when children dramatize their pain in order to evoke sympathy from

---

[53] Colin E. Gunton, *The Actuality of Atonement: A Study of Metaphor, Rationality and the Christian Tradition* (Grand Rapids: Eerdmans, 1989) 126.

[54] Isa 1:11-15; 66:3; Hos 3:4; 4:8-12; 6:4-9; 8:11-13; 9:4; Amos 4:4-5; 5:21-25; Mic 6:6-8.

[55] Pss 40:6-9; 50:9-14, 23; 51:16-17; 69:30-31.

[56] Gunton, *Actuality of Atonement*, 118, 136.

[57] Ibid., 51–52.

[58] I call this "Spiritualization Level Two" in *Background*, 48–49, 56, and *Problems*, 22, 24, 61–62, 87–88. See the surrounding material for the other ways in which "spiritualization" is used by scholars.

their parents or to provoke punishment of siblings. Such manipulative practices persist into adulthood, but we usually disguise our motives, even from ourselves. The whole discourse of "sacrifice" needs to be subjected to a hermeneutic of suspicion, as it embraces motives both selfish and unselfish and is used to make statements about politics, war, religion, economics, and family life, using concepts from one realm to interpret another and to misrepresent one's motives as purely unselfish.

"The metaphor of sacrifice . . . brings us closest . . . to the very heart of [God's] being."[59] Of course, by "sacrifice" Gunton means endless giving, but that is not what ritual sacrifice really was. Such spiritualization is a common homiletical strategy, of course, and may be useful for stirring a congregation toward higher motives, but it glosses over the manipulative motives inherent in sacrificial thinking. When selfish motives are disguised, they are perpetuated.

Gunton has a strong ethical sense, as do many of those who strive to express atonement theologies in ways that are morally palatable. He speaks of restoration and reestablishment of right relations with God and of the Spirit of God enabling the world to become perfected.[60] He opposes "the objectionable notion that Jesus is . . . punished by God in our stead."[61] He issues many cautions about the legal metaphor of atonement and is aware that it is dangerous "to read that metaphor literally";[62] Anselm, for instance, takes "too literally the allusion to ransom."[63] Yet Gunton still regards sin as "an indelible stain" or a "burden,"[64] speaking of "pollution cleansed" and of "an objective weight of transgression" needing "removal."[65] Sin as a cleansable stain or removable burden perpetuates the metaphysics underlying the ancient ritual. These literalizing images reveal an archaic, superstitious underpinning, thus weakening the ethical reinterpretation of sacrifice.

Gunton's spiritualizing effort requires that he deny that there is any penal substitution in the biblical concepts. Thus he warns against construing sacrifice "with the aid of penal imagery, in terms of God's visiting upon the human Jesus the penalties owed by others"; inconsistently,

---

[59] Gunton, *Actuality of Atonement*, 197.

[60] Ibid., 167.

[61] Ibid., 161–62.

[62] Ibid., 165.

[63] Ibid., 88. "A relative failure to link the incarnation with creation and human regeneration" (99).

[64] Ibid., 164–65.

[65] Ibid., 161–62; cf. 119.

however, he is happy to speak of "the sacrificial gift . . . the metaphorical transfer . . . the one reordering sacrifice."[66] This is an attempt to simultaneously preserve primitive mystery and advancing ethics. In such an approach, mystery will always win out over ethics. We see this, for instance, in his rejection of any interpretation that places a premium "on the response of the believer" as "Pelagianism."[67]

Gunton thinks to eliminate any notion of penal substitution by saying "the gift . . . is . . . the voluntary self-giving of Jesus."[68] Evidently, *voluntary* giving expunges any allegation of propitiation or substitution. There is no "punitive substitution" because "the death of Jesus was a free and voluntary human act."[69] It was God-initiated sacrifice, not human-initiated.[70] But this in no way distinguishes Christian from pagan belief. All sacrificial ideologies claim to have a divine origin. Divine initiative in ritual is as much a truism of Tikopia[71] mythology as it is of Levitical. Ian Bradley observes that what leads Gunton to "over-stress the voluntary nature of Jesus' sacrifice [is a] desire to avoid any suggestion of propitiation."[72]

In his later writing Gunton seems to promote a substitutionary concept: "we must, however qualifiedly, speak of penal exchange, if not of penal substitution in the old sense. . . . [S]omething is given in place of and for the sake of the other. Here, the Son of God takes the sinner's place."[73] In the earlier book he gives a mixed message about substitution, resisting the "rationalistic theory of . . . penal substitution" and the idea of "a substitutionary killing,"[74] yet saying that Jesus "must be said either to *represent* or to be a *substitute* for the rest of us. . . . The 'for us' of the cross and resurrection must *include*, though it is not exhausted by, an

---

[66] Colin Gunton, "Christ the Sacrifice: Aspects of the Language and Imagery of the Bible," in L. D. Hurst and N. T. Wright, eds., *The Glory of Christ in the New Testament: Studies in Christology in Memory of George Bradford Caird* (Oxford: Clarendon Press, 1987) 238.

[67] Gunton, *Actuality of Atonement*, 18.

[68] Gunton, "Christ the Sacrifice," 238.

[69] Gunton, *Actuality of Atonement*, 124.

[70] Ibid., 126–27; cf. C. F. D. Moule: "precisely because the initiative is God's, it becomes impossible any longer to think of him as requiring to be propitiated" (in idem, *Essays in New Testament Interpretation* [Cambridge: Cambridge University Press, 1982] 238; cf. 289).

[71] W. Richard Comstock, *The Study of Religion and Primitive Religions* (New York: Harper & Row, 1971) 37.

[72] Ian Bradley, *Power of Sacrifice* (London: Darton, Longman & Todd, 1995) 114.

[73] Colin E. Gunton, "Towards a Theology of Reconciliation," in idem, ed., *The Theology of Reconciliation* (London: T & T Clark, 2003) 170–71.

[74] Gunton, *Actuality of Atonement*, 16, 134.

'instead of.'"[75] This reinstates substitution. What is at issue is the motivation of God; Gunton does not want to concede that there are differing concepts of God behind different NT passages, or that there is contradiction between God as loving father and God as sacrifice-demander.

There is no doubt that Colin Gunton is a high-minded individual who wishes people to avoid base and manipulative ideas of God. His strongest point is to warn against separating Jesus from God in terms of motives; God and Jesus work together in the supreme act of *giving.* Thus his theory stands or falls on the question of whether atonement concepts can successfully avoid dividing Jesus from God in terms of loving generosity. But the whole logic of atonement hinges on some "price" or "penalty" being paid by the Son to the Father. At the very least, atonement assumes the kindness of God placating the judgment of God, although this is rarely admitted nowadays by defenders of atonement. Paul, too, wants to minimize or deny this concept, but he uses metaphors that imply exactly this. Because of his concern to "by all means save some" (1 Cor 9:22), Paul was willing to use dubious (but effective) metaphors, and we struggle today with the contradictory implications of his teachings.

Moule and Others: Innocent Blood

Another attempt to allow sacrifice a smooth transition into unselfish giving is made by the high-minded scholar C. F. D. Moule. He correctly notes that "the word 'sacrifice' has already lost its cultic connotation, and means simply the surrender of something precious," but incorrectly says that NT sacrificial language "may be translated without essential loss into the language of a different analogy, namely, that of expenditure, of giving in a costly way."[76] To describe this transfer as being "without loss" is to disguise the fact that it comes with substantial *gain,* that is, *alteration:* bestowing a false dignity on sacrifice by disguising its superstitious metaphysics and its selfish motives. He argues that "sacrifice" is now used in a noncultic way to mean unselfish and costly service, but he paints over the manipulative psychology that underlies even this moralizing meaning. People frequently offer tales of their personal "sacrifice" to get others to feel guilty or obligated. Sacrifice as costly payment is thought to have persuasive power over others, including God. Moule

---

[75] Ibid., 161, 165. Jesus is both substitute and representative (166).

[76] C. F. D. Moule, "Preaching the Atonement," *Epworth Review* 10 (1983) 71.

is right to repudiate the notion of paying off God as "crudely propitiatory,"[77] but he does admit: "It is difficult . . . to use the word [sacrifice]
without its implying a propitiatory intention."[78] Here he lets the cat out
of the bag: sacrifice entails manipulation. The logic of sacrifice is manipulative, always looking for a desired outcome.

Moule attaches the noble idea of personal cost to the barbaric one of
advantage gained through sacrifice, a complex strategy commonly encountered in Christian theology through the ages. The metaphysics of
the ancient ritual is preserved in the spiritualized sacrifice idea. Even in
moral discussions, then, a tinge of superstition must creep in, as when
Moule says, "only by completely innocent suffering can forgiveness be
completely proffered."[79] This is a blending of moral and magical thinking. I do not think that Moule is aware of the dark undercurrents of this
belief in the efficacy of "innocent suffering." Of course, he is following
a well-trodden path in atonement thinking. Augustine of Hippo had
seen innocent blood as carrying a kind of legal tender: "The shedding
of innocent blood has blotted out all the sins of the guilty; so great a price
paid has redeemed all the captives."[80] All the violence of sacrificial per-
suasion is rendered "spiritual" and covered over with sentimentality
when one speaks of the power of "innocent blood." Is there not a chilling
undercurrent to this concept? Does it not pose a threat to the innocent?

Moule is certainly correct to point out that "juridical terms . . . drive
a wedge between the Persons of the Trinity,"[81] but he does not succeed
in his attempt to utterly banish juridical concepts from the soteriologies
of Paul and the author of Hebrews. His mission is noble: "to remove
from our minds any crudely propitiatory conception of the sacrifice of
Christ,"[82] but even calling it a sacrifice carries forward a strategy for
persuading the gods. Sacrificial thinking itself is the problem. The appeal
to "sacrifice" communicates all the old and manipulative meanings, no
matter how many new and ethicized meanings are attached to it.

Moule says the sacrifice of Christ works because of Christ's "willing
obedience" and "yearning love."[83] But again Moule's honesty lets us

---

[77] C. F. D. Moule, *The Sacrifice of Christ*. FBBS 12 (Philadelphia: Fortress Press, 1964) 35.
[78] Moule, "Preaching the Atonement," 71.
[79] Ibid., 74.
[80] *Enarr. In Ps.* 129, 3, from Eugène Portalie, *A Guide to the Thought of Saint Augustine*,
trans. Ralph Bastian (Chicago: Henry Regnery, 1960) 167.
[81] Moule, *Sacrifice of Christ*, 34.
[82] Ibid., 35.
[83] Ibid., 14–15.

glimpse the weakness in his argument. He lets us see the element of bargaining or negotiating with God: "Jesus is the negotiator of a new covenant ([Heb] 8:6; 12:24)."[84] This, again, is manipulative. Moule would rebut me by saying that the analogy has been "lifted off the . . . level of ritual acts on to the level of personal dealings. . . . Jesus as representative man fulfilling that destiny of obedience and harmony with God."[85] What I am calling "manipulative," Moule would call "relational." I admit that it is possible to see this glass as half full or half empty, but it is hardly possible to see it as completely full, as a consistent and noble concept with no ethical problems, no theological primitivism, no psychological undertow.

Another perceptive scholar falls under the "innocent blood" spell.[86] Although he acknowledges the arguments of feminists against using atonement doctrine to ask the downtrodden to continue suffering, William Placher ends up repeating the old blood magic: "The bloody body of Christ reminds us of the price that was paid for our freedom. . . . Christ is our sacrifice. His blood transforms us into people who can once again come into the presence of the holy God."[87]

If access to the holy God requires innocent blood, then "holy" retains ancient notions of a remote and violent deity. This chilling concept of blood magic is still widespread, even in scholarly arguments: "Because he [is] innocent his blood is the infinitely valuable means of atonement."[88]

Behind such ideas stand not the God with whom we can converse (Isa 1:18) nor the loving God who runs to forgive us, like the Prodigal Son's father (Luke 15:20), but the hungry and dangerous gods of ancient times. Isaiah calls for good-doing and faithful conversing with God. Jesus promises a generous welcome from God for all who turn back to God. The moral change in the individual enables reconnection with God. But anything that involves moral decision is labeled "Pelagian" by atonement theorists, for whom the saving moment is at the crucifixion; all that believers can do is to *believe* a certain interpretation of that event. Salvation, then, becomes entirely an ideological matter, the act of subscribing to an *interpretation*. In this approach to salvation, ideology suffocates

---

[84] Ibid., 15.

[85] Ibid., 15.

[86] William C. Placher, *Jesus the Savior: The Meaning of Jesus Christ for Christian Faith* (Louisville: Westminster John Knox, 2001) 116, 120, 126–32.

[87] Ibid., 149, 137.

[88] Peter Stuhlmacher, *Paul's Letter to the Romans: A Commentary* (Louisville: Westminster John Knox, 1994) 61.

ethics. Consequently, no religion has been so meticulous and judgmental about beliefs and creeds as Christianity. How many honest believers have been interrogated and tortured about their beliefs by supposed guardians of Christian doctrine?

All concepts of the saving efficacy of "the bloody body of Christ"[89] involve the notion of something magical taking place at the cross. What magic was there in this atrocity? God's attitude was not changed by this shameful act of violence. There was nothing beautiful, wonderful, or salvific in the torturing and killing of the Messiah. Christians fall under a mythmaking spell when they give in to the primitive tendency to attribute everything to God, failing to distinguish between what God intends and what God allows. People tend to blame God for every catastrophic event: "Who sinned, this man or his parents, that he was born blind?" (John 9:2); "Do you think that because these Galileans suffered in this way they were worse sinners than all other Galileans? No" (Luke 13:2-3). It is primitive thinking to believe that catastrophes, deformities, and diseases are personal expressions of the wrath of God. This is a failure of religious philosophy (see "Religious and Philosophic Progress," below).

4.1B Is Healing Power in the Cross?

What is it about "innocent blood" that is thought to be so spiritually effective? Is it not the imagined persuasive power of painful giving? *Surely* God will be moved by *this* suffering! Whether the "innocent blood" is pictured as having a sort of commercial value or a magical cleansing power, some benefit is *obtained* from the divine level. The persuasive power of martyrdom operates by the same logic. The perfect innocence of the martyr is efficacious. The martyr's sacrifice is the unparalleled offering that persuades the Deity to "withdraw your wrath."[90] The appeal of martyrdom, besides its exaltation of courage and loyalty, is the intuitive belief that martyrdom has persuasive power.

There is a certain idolatry of the cross going on here, where the cross becomes more fundamental than the Savior, where Jesus only gets his legitimacy from "the cross." I doubt that most authors are aware of the idolatrous implications of their thinking when they say things like this:

---

[89] Placher, *Jesus the Savior*, 149.
[90] And similar phrases: Exod 32:12; Deut 13:17; 2 Chr 30:8; Ps 85:2-7; 4 *Macc.* 4:11.

"If one cannot find a way to confess the saving power of the cross, then Jesus becomes irrelevant and the church has no good news."[91] This is to say that without the cross, Jesus is nothing. This completely negates the saving actions he performed during his lifetime. It also ignores *who* Jesus was and is, before, during, and after he came to earth. Christ, not the cross, is the Savior.

Vicarious cleansing and symbolic payment were not the means for approaching God recommended by Jesus himself. Jesus said the Father knows what we need before we ask and *wants* to give us good things.[92] In fact, we can get what we need from the Father himself: "I do not say to you that I will ask the Father on your behalf; for the Father himself loves you" (John 16:26-27). No payment is needed. Do we have to come with blood when we approach our earthly fathers? Neither does our heavenly Father require such. Fear and superstition fuel those beliefs.

Jesus says straightforwardly that the faith response opens up a channel between God and human, enabling healing and forgiveness. To the hemorrhaging woman and the grateful leper, people who suffered as much from social ostracism as from physical affliction, he says: "your faith has made you well" (Luke 8:48; 17:19). Their perceived impurity was not cured with any ritual or with any substitutionary message. What healed these people was the presence of Jesus' inherent creative power and their ability to tap into that power through their faith-reach. We see this in the story of the man with the withered hand; it was not only Jesus' healing power but the man's faith-action that brought about the healing; he responded to the call to "Stretch out your hand" (Matt 12:13). Again, when Jesus spoke to the paralytic and the faithful people carrying him, "Jesus saw their faith" and so was able to say, "Take heart, son; your sins are forgiven" (Matt 9:2). "Take heart" encourages the person to exercise his own powers of faith, thus enabling the healing energy to flow from Jesus, who is the embodiment of God. The man *exercised faith* when he cooperated with Jesus' instruction to "stand up and walk" (9:5-6). All of this takes place without any substitutionary death.

If we believe the NT report that Jesus is the creator or cocreator of this world (it was "through" him that God "created the worlds," Heb 1:2; "all things were made through him," John 1:3 (RSV); all things were created "in him" and "through" him (Col 1:16; 1 Cor 8:6), we should not be surprised that he has creative power in him. It is not astounding that

---

[91] Schmiechen, *Saving Power*, 1.
[92] Matt 6:8; 7:7-11; Luke 12:28-32; John 16:23-27; cf. Jas 1:17.

he should be able to heal. This has nothing to do with his death but with the power he had before our world was made, power that he retained when he took on flesh and lived as a mortal.

If salvation came only as a consequence of his crucifixion, Jesus certainly forgot to mention this to those people who came to him seeking salvation. They must have gone away unsaved—but then, why did he say, "your faith has saved you"?

Certain atonement formulas imply that the Savior has no saving power but only *the cross* has it. Further, they present creative power as coming not from the Creator but from the significance of his "blood." This is an instance of allowing the symbol to displace the reality, even making the symbol into an idol. Reverence for "the cross" and "the blood" sells out Jewish monotheism to the highest pagan bidder: superstition about the magical power of innocent blood—the greatest magic of all being the blood of the *most* innocent person.

If the innocent Son *had* to be murdered before God would save, then God is either not fully powerful or not fully good, being either *unable* to offer forgiveness until a certain ritual killing is carried out, or *unwilling* to offer forgiveness until that victim is provided, making God either weak or cruel, either easily manipulated or corrupt. Nor does it help to couch it in terms of a ransom payment, which suggests bribery. This outrages the moral reactions that were implanted in us by God. It is crazy-making theology, producing suicidal saints and rage-dominated parental figures who think they are helping their children when they beat them.[93]

Each of the basic ingredients of popular atonement thinking suffocates some essential aspect of theology. Recompense as an immovable necessity suffocates God's compassion and healing power. Vicarious substitution negates justice (no honest court would allow it). The supposed ritual power of innocent blood reduces the free will of God, suggesting that God *must* respond to this ritual.

Our traditional doctrines of atonement, as spelled out by Augustine, Gregory the Great, Anselm, Luther, and Calvin, offer a mixed message about God, and the evidence is seen in the severe conflicts experienced by serious religious people. Punishment is only avoided by an undeserved rescue. Therefore gratitude is colored with guilt; confession grants only

---

[93] The *mother* can be the raging and abusive parent, as experienced by Alice Miller, the great psychologist and writer who exposed the harmfulness of beating children (*Banished Knowledge*, 7, 23–24, 76, 179).

temporary relief; repentance brings only short-lived reform; liturgy stimulates but a passing feeling of release. The mentality of shame that underlies atonement teaching will always reassert itself. In some people, atonement doctrines stimulate guilt (the feeling of having done something wrong); in others they foster shame (the feeling of *being* something wrong). Teachings that *humble* may be necessary, but teachings that *humiliate* are deeply damaging. Election is also a problematic concept: What comfort is there in being specially favored if others are specially *un*favored? Is God unfair?

The abuse-shaped attitudes and deformed religious notions of those brought up in sacrificial cultures have now become the attitudes and doctrines of those brought up believing in *metaphorical* atonement. The underlying sacrificial superstition gets perpetuated and partially spiritualized. The doctrine replaces the *actual* sacrificial ritual but not its underlying fears. These fears get acted out in the household, and children are on the receiving end.

There is a terrible irony here: the world's most advanced religion also has the most advanced stage of spiritualized superstition. Christianity has taken atonement as far as it can go and now stands at a crossroads where it must choose between advancing with some uncertainty without that outmoded symbol or stagnating by clinging to a symbol that can no longer be advanced.

Attempts to advance the symbol by filling it with postmodernist content will be examined next.

4.2A Postmodernist Orthodox Views

Boersma: God Must Be Violent

Hans Boersma offers a theory that tries to provide a place for both violence and hospitality in the doings of God, although "violence" seems to include any kind of exclusion, not necessarily with physical force. Boersma repeatedly asserts that "hospitality cannot be practiced without violence."[94] "Because God's hospitality takes place within a history already marred by human violence, his hospitality cannot be pure or universal."[95] Apparently the same constraints that apply to humans ("every

---

[94] Hans Boersma, *Violence, Hospitality, and the Cross* (Grand Rapids: Baker, 2004) 154.
[95] Ibid., 84.

human act is already embedded in a context infested with violence")[96] apply to God ("God's entry in restricted and inhospitable surroundings required the use of violence").[97] God is evidently no exception to the rule that "violence is inscribed in the very nature of things and cannot ever be avoided."[98]

Having God be unable to transcend the created order is clearly a failure of theology, nor is it just a problem of terminology, although Boersma *does* make the term "violence" serve a dual purpose. One is the normal meaning; the other refers to any kind of social exclusion or dominance, a meaning given to it by Derrida. Boersma often intends "the violence of exclusion" (28) when he says "violence," but at other times he means any use of physical force—even forcefully stopping someone from committing suicide is violent (46). The reader has to study the context and even then sometimes must guess at which meaning of "violence" is intended.

In fact, this ambiguity enables Boersma to pronounce Calvinist-sounding maxims that actually have postmodernist and relativizing content. While he criticizes Calvin, who "draws divine violence into the heart of God,"[99] Boersma uses Calvinist phrasing to make many of his points, as when speaking of Paul's excluding those who wanted to exclude the Gentiles: "God's hospitality in Christ needs an edge of violence to ensure the welcome of humanity" (93). If he really means the violence of social exclusion here, why confuse the issue with these perverse maxims about the supposed necessity of "violence"?

Despite the atonement language, Boersma really has dropped the transactional notion of atonement without stressing that he has done so. Instead, he uses certain atonement-sounding language while articulating a Derridean notion of the guiltiness of all human group formation. So guilt lies at the basis even of this atonement rhetoric!

This is a tragic result, since a shaming doctrine was not Boersma's intention at all. He offers a very useful discussion of Irenaeus' incarnational soteriology—Jesus' "recapitulation" or repair of each stage of human life by his living through it,[100] persuading believers to learn from

---

[96] Ibid., 34 n. 34.

[97] Ibid., 37 n. 46.

[98] Ibid., 35.

[99] Ibid., 56; he offers some objection to the usual concept of "vicarious substitution" (122 n. 24, 158, 183 n. 7).

[100] Ibid., 122–26; from *Against Heresies* II.22.4-6; III.18.7, 19.1; IV.38.2; V.1.2.

"our Teacher . . . receiving increase from the perfect One,"[101] but there is not enough of this hopeful and constructive theology to undo the damage done by his peculiar yoking of relativistic Derrida to absolutizing Calvin.

Milbank: Atonement as Forgiveness

John Milbank offers a stunning and profound interpretation, recognizing that a cultic concept of atonement that remains purely doctrinal and extrinsic has no moral usefulness, does not transform the believer: "so it is pointless to approach incarnation and atonement primarily as revealed propositions."[102] They are, rather, metaphors and narrative devices, Milbank argues, and are meant to stimulate Christian ethics. The danger of a purely "cultic" reading of atonement is that it calls for something apart from human forgiveness, and "if Christ's death is necessary in addition to the practice of forgiveness, then monstrous consequences ensue," for it would make the perpetrators of violence "the necessary agents of redemption"[103] and so involve God in both an atrocity and an absurdity.

Milbank argues that "metaphors of atonement—'ransom,' 'sacrifice,' 'victory'—are *not* to be taken realistically, as . . . an invisible eternal transaction between God and humanity"; rather, Jesus' death "*inaugura[tes]* the 'political' practice of forgiveness. . . . [B]ecause forgiveness is itself atonement, it follows that [it] must be continuously renewed," and it is Christ who set this "renewed mode of life," this "repetition of an atoning practice," in motion.[104] So "atonement must be drastically reconceived from an ecclesiological vantage point"; it has to involve "real transformation,"[105] because the difficult process of forgiveness really does change those who participate in it. "How can mere belief in . . . atonement be uniquely transformative for the individual?"[106]

Milbank removes atonement from the realm of soteriology, transferring it wholly to the realm of ethics, with a consequent transformation

---

[101] Boersma, *Violence*, 129; from *AH* V.1.1.

[102] John Milbank, "The Name of Jesus: Incarnation, Atonement, Ecclesiology," *Modern Theology* 7 (1991) 315. Reprinted in his *The Word Made Strange: Theology, Language, Culture* (Oxford: Blackwell, 1997) 148. I will cite *Word Made Strange* from now on for any article collected in that book.

[103] Milbank, *Word Made Strange*, 159.

[104] Ibid., 161.

[105] Ibid., 162.

[106] Ibid., 148.

of character and of sociality. Christians need to participate in the same process of nonviolent giving that Jesus dramatized, and this, Milbank argues, is the heart of Paul's teaching:

> "Participation in atonement," the "filling up what is lacking in the sufferings of Christ for the sake of his body, the Church" (Col. 1:24) . . . 2 Cor. 1:3-12[:] Not only does this passage make clear that every Christian must personally pass through, and not merely acknowledge, the cross, it also indicates that these sufferings are of "consolatory" or atoning value to the community.[107]

Milbank's view has an obvious ethical advantage over Lutheran doctrines of atonement (as he readily notices), but also over Augustinian and Anselmian understandings (although he denies this, arguing that "for Anselm there is no question of anything being received as a compensatory offering by God").[108] Milbank notes that atonement, treated as a propositional truth, simply does not work. Rather, it works only when it is practiced, first by the one truly innocent sufferer (Christ) and then by those who accept Christ's Spirit. Atonement is our assignment and our privilege, growing out of our recognition of God's generosity and the certainty of our eventual vindication.

Milbank goes so far as to articulate an antisacrificial understanding of atonement: "The New Testament does not speak of Jesus' death as a sacrifice in the rabbinic sense of a death atoning for sins. . . . St. Paul therefore speaks not of the offering of Christ to the Father, with whom he is really identical, but, instead, of our dying to sin . . . *with Christ*."[109] Milbank understands this atoning project to be about the business of defeating the powers of violence, not of paying off God, and it means an end to sacrifice:

> If any "ransom" is offered by Christ, then it seems indeed that for St. Paul, as the Fathers divulged, it is granted to the chthonic gods who are really demons . . . (Gal. 4:3-4). . . . Yet Paul's point is that these powers are nothing . . . hence such a sacrifice becomes, in Christian terms, absurd. Only in a comical sense was Christ, strictly speaking, a sacrifice. In a serious sense he was an effective sacrifice because he overcame sacrifice once and for all.[110]

---

[107] Ibid., 184.

[108] Ibid., 163.

[109] John Milbank, *Being Reconciled: Ontology and Pardon*. Radical Orthodoxy Series (London: Routledge, 2003) 99.

[110] Ibid., 99–100.

"Sacrifice" seems to fit within the realm of violence, then. This resonates with the views of antisacrificial thinkers from Micah to Empedocles to René Girard. The ethical outcome is one with strongly pacifistic tendencies:

> The divine answer to the original human refusal of his gift is not to demand sacrifice—of which he has no need—but to go on giving. . . . Christ's abandonment offers no compensation to God. . . . It is the same for the *Epistle to the Hebrews:* sacrifice implies multiplicity, repetition, appeasement, whereas Christ the true Priest puts an end to sacrifice.[111]

Like Gunton, Milbank eliminates all selfishness from biblical ideas of sacrifice, attributing them only to pagan sacrifice. He has a highly spiritualizing explanation of the Aqedah, saying that the unreasonable demand for the son, with the surprise ending of returning the son alive, shows how generous God is; God "demands no share—he rather demands all, in order that he may give all, again."[112] We know that there is a tragic demand made upon honest people who refuse, at any cost, to betray principles. Loyalty to principle must mean losing one's life, either symbolically or actually. But it is the corrupt world, not God, that demands sacrifice. Perhaps a spiritualizing hermeneutic that distorts some OT narratives is *necessary* in order to practice real obedience to Jesus. It is certainly an improvement on Genesis 22 to say that God never demands sacrifice and never calls for violence but does ask for total surrender.

Milbank draws our attention to the ethic of self-giving that is embodied in Jesus' self-giving, an ethic we need to adopt even though the world will not understand such unselfishness. Unless we take up our cross—and joyously—we have not understood our Master. But if the church will practice joyous self-giving it can help to demonstrate that "violence is precisely that which lacks all power."[113]

Atonement, for Milbank, is truth-loyalty and affirmation of Jesus' resurrection, followed by final receipt of one's own resurrection as gift. This seems to be a complete redefinition of atonement in terms of the essentials of Christian faith. Atonement as sacrifice, as payment, as God-determined penalty, is a misinterpretation. Milbank argues for an intriguing option: that the whole concept of atonement can be reinterpreted in a fully orthodox way, without resort to literal-minded substitutionary ideas. The loving intention of God is not altered by the cowardice of

---

[111] Ibid., 100.
[112] John Milbank, "Stories of Sacrifice," *Modern Theology* 12 (1996) 53.
[113] Milbank, *Word Made Strange*, 165.

those who kill the principled people; God is always giving and forgiving. There is no payment here. There is only Creation and re-creation.

However, it is precisely on this and related points, that Milbank is criticized by Michael Horton, who is not pleased with Milbank's

> conflation of Christ and church, church and cosmos, Christ's atonement and ours. . . . Radical Orthodoxy seems overly nervous about distinctions. The "one" very nearly swallows the "many" whole. . . . "The gospels can be read, not as the story of Jesus, but as the story of the (re)foundation of a new city" . . . (*Word Made Strange*, 150). Ecclesiology swallows Christology.[114]

This is partly legitimate. The bodies of Milbank's articles are lengthy and erudite, yet he rushes to these lofty conclusions about forgiveness, new community, the ethics of resurrection, without addressing certain issues. His work is genuinely Christian but highly elastic and innovative, and hardly as Augustinian or Thomist as he claims. But Horton's opinion that Milbank's approach is "metaphysical-ontological-speculative," while the Reformation's is "ethical-historical-eschatological,"[115] seems unfair. Horton attacks Milbank when he criticizes "a crudely 'mythological' and 'penal substitutionary' interpretation . . . which imports . . . later doctrinal speculation,"[116] but Milbank's critique is both ethical and historical (he is criticizing a view that would sacralize Judas' act of betrayal), while Horton's objection looks doctrinaire and narrow.

Horton's last contrast (speculative vs. eschatological) is refuted by Milbank's insight into deification. Milbank is one of the few western theologians who grasps the significance of deification—the promise of the transformation of the believer (Rom 12:2; 2 Cor 3:18); "to be conformed to the image of his Son" (Rom 8:29); becoming like "the man of heaven" (1 Cor 15:49). Though he does not cite these passages, Milbank understands this deification eschatology.[117] He builds on Thomas Aquinas, who "espouses ontologically strong notions of deification. . . . [T]he

---

[114] Michael S. Horton, "Participation and Covenant," in James K. A. Smith and James H. Olthuis, eds., *Radical Orthodoxy and the Reformed Tradition: Creation, Covenant, and Participation* (Grand Rapids: Baker Academic, 2005) 129.

[115] Horton, "Participation and Covenant," 132.

[116] Ibid., 129; Milbank, *Word Made Strange*, 159.

[117] Three recent titles on the topic are Stephen Finlan and Vladimir Kharlamov, eds., *Theosis: Deification in Christian Tradition*. PTMS 52 (Eugene, OR: Wipf & Stock, 2006); Norman Russell, *The Doctrine of Deification in the Greek Patristic Tradition* (Oxford: Oxford University Press, 2005); and Michael Christensen and Jeffery Wittung, eds., *Partakers of the Divine Nature: The History and Development of Deification in the Christian Traditions* (Madison, NJ: Fairleigh Dickinson University Press, 2006).

Incarnation . . . brings about . . . the conjoining of humanity to divinity."[118] Humanity receives new spiritual abilities as a result of the incarnation, and we are able to participate in the divine recycling of love. Western theology, having become obsessed with the sinfulness of humanity, has all but forgotten this teaching (even though Augustine, Calvin, and the early Luther each endorsed some version of it); Eastern Orthodoxy never lost sight of the doctrine.

Deification is a nontransactional concept of salvation, one that entails ethical and spiritual growth. Milbank is drawn to this kind of idea. Even when "reconciliation" is the subject, he says that the incarnation does not "bring about this reconciliation for God, but [makes] it effective for us"—we are being reeducated in the ways of true penitence.[119] We have to learn how to go on giving despite rejection, just as God has always done. "Divine redemption is not God's forgiving us, but rather his giving us the gift of the capacity for forgiveness. . . . Christological forgiveness is . . . only the sustained giving of the original gift."[120]

Milbank's redefinition (or rediscovery) of atonement means, therefore, a redefinition of "ethics, not as one-way sacrifice, but as total surrender for renewed reception,"[121] and "to be ethical therefore is to believe in the Resurrection, and somehow to participate in it."[122]

This tendency to radically redefine Christian doctrines (replacing atonement with ethics, after he had already replaced ethics with "gift" and resurrection-faith) has some appeal, but it is based on a series of distortions. Jesus gets absorbed into the church and the forgiveness process he initiated. Apart from the community "he cannot be given any particular content."[123] Jesus turns out to be "simply the founder, the beginning, the first of many."[124] This is a weakened christology.[125] In fact, Milbank's "orthodoxy" is deeply romantic (despite his revulsion with most romanticism) and ethical (despite his denial that Christian ethics are based on right and wrong). There is a heavy dose of "cultural pessi-

---

[118] Milbank, *Being Reconciled*, 66–67.

[119] Ibid., 64–65, citing *Summa Theologica* III. Q. 1 a 3 ad 1, and *Summa Contra Gentiles* IV.42 (4).

[120] Milbank, *Being Reconciled*, 62, 68.

[121] Ibid., 161.

[122] Ibid., 148.

[123] Milbank, *Word Made Strange*, 152.

[124] Ibid., 150.

[125] Effectively argued by Hans Boersma, "Being Reconciled: Atonement as the Ecclesio-Christological Practice of Forgiveness in John Milbank," in *Radical Orthodoxy and the Reformed Tradition*, 196.

mism"[126] in Milbank, and it comes through in his highly cultured condemnation of modern culture, his densely academic attack on academic social theory.

4.2B Postmodern Cynicism

We noticed that Boersma's theory that God must partake of violence seems to lose sight of the transcendence of God. This is not true about Milbank, who sees transcendence in Jesus' and God's rejection of, and conquest of, violence. Yet there is an ironic similarity between the postmodernist Boersma, who uses traditional language, and the traditionalist Milbank, whose method is postmodernist. Each is deeply skeptical of the human ability to reason about God; Boersma holds to the idea of a covenant community but otherwise seems content with relativism in religious knowledge; Milbank seeks clear religious truth and an ideal and uncompromising religious community.

Boersma's God is willing to exercise violence on groups and individuals who threaten the covenant community—or does "violence" just mean "exclusion from the group"? Milbank's God suffers violence in order to show the powerlessness of violence and creates a community that is based on forgiveness. Boersma allows the hospitality of voluntary suffering, while Milbank speaks of a "perfect because innocent suffering,"[127] yet neither wants to defend the basic propositions of violent atonement theology. Still, both intellectualize around the arena of sacrifice. Milbank's vision is motivated by eschatological hope but presumes a thoroughly evil society that will not respond to the truth. Boersma defends the necessity of some exclusive practices and expresses hope only when he remembers to focus on the transformational vision of Irenaeus, not when he leans toward the extreme relativism of Derrida. Both are fairly cynical about secular society and culture.

Douglas Hedley says that Milbank's hostility to the Enlightenment critique of religion goes so far that he "will not recognize a perspective outside of the theological."[128] Milbank, he claims, is always trying "to

---

[126] Jonathan Chaplin, "Suspended Communities or Covenant Communities? Reformed Reflections on the Social Thought of Radical Orthodoxy," in *Radical Orthodoxy and the Reformed Tradition*, 174. Chaplin criticizes the Radical Orthodox attempt to make the church the basis for all social institutions.

[127] Milbank, *Word Made Strange*, 164.

[128] Douglas Hedley, "Should Divinity Overcome Metaphysics? Reflections on John Milbank's Theology beyond Secular Reason and Confessions of a Cambridge Platonist," in *Journal of Religion* 80 (2000) 272.

rescue the Christian theological tradition from any contagion of 'Greek' metaphysics. . . . This expunging the Christian theological tradition of its speculative heritage is as violent as it is implausible."[129] Greek thought had seen reason "as the divine within man," and Hedley claims that Milbank rejects this, seeing God as wholly other,[130] but he goes too far here. In fact Milbank's appropriation of Aquinas stresses human "participation in Being and goodness. . . . To have some knowledge of virtue, of perfection, is imperfectly to know one's humanity."[131]

Still, we have to say that Boersma and Milbank fall into a similar dualistic trap, posing Enlightenment modernism as the root of all evil, and on this point I think Hedley is correct: "The postmodern attack on foundations seems to justify the ultimately Barthian refusal to engage in dialogue with the secular."[132] There is a certain irony in Milbank's erudite attack on human reason, when one needs at least two Ph.D.s to understand some of his sentences. It is an elitist critique of elitism. Perhaps that is the only way to get elites to listen, but it means that Milbank is primarily talking to the academy, not to the church, despite his wish to make the church an ideal community.

4.3 Options on Forgiveness and Wrath

Moule's Insight

Whenever atonement is discussed, issues of divine justice and forgiveness are raised. This should lead to a discussion of human justice and forgiveness. C. F. D. Moule raises the subject, showing that Christian forgiveness has nothing to do with retaliation or "payback." Christian forgiveness never embraces any form of revenge or calls for any kind of satisfaction that goes beyond the purposes of education or deterrence.[133] "The motive of forgiveness is always to heal and to restore the offender and never to 'take it out of him.'"[134] Much Christian atonement theology has obscured the meaning of forgiveness by importing notions of pun-

---

[129] Hedley, "Should Divinity Overcome," 274, where he also points out that Milbank's hero, Augustine, is himself an upholder of just that "metaphysics of inwardness" Milbank claims to repudiate.

[130] Hedley, "Should Divinity Overcome," 273.

[131] Milbank, *Word Made Strange*, 15–16.

[132] Hedley, "Should Divinity Overcome," 274.

[133] C. F. D. Moule, "The Theology of Forgiveness," in Norman Autton, ed., *From Fear to Faith: Studies of Suffering and Wholeness* (London: S.P.C.K., 1971) 63.

[134] Ibid., 66.

ishment: "A crude doctrine of a feudal God who demands a penalty to be undergone by Jesus Christ as satisfaction, before he can forgive the sins of mankind, is monstrous and clearly unacceptable."[135]

He notes that some passages in the Bible do speak of punishment or retaliation, sometimes with considerable violence, and mentions "the retributive motive" in Romans 2:6-11; Matthew 13:42, 50; and the book of Revelation,[136] but the usual emphasis in the NT is not retaliation but rescue and repair: "God is a God who puts the wicked right" and who goes to great lengths to accomplish this, "who exercises his sovereign creative power by suffering, not by causing to suffer."[137] When Paul exhorts to social punishment, says Christopher Marshall, "the intention of the punishment is to reclaim the offender, restore relationships, and bring healing to the victim."[138]

On the human level forgiveness needs to be followed by moral re-education, usually for both parties; it is not meant to be a technique that enables misbehavior to continue. As Moule writes, "real forgiveness is undoubtedly costly to the forgiver. . . . A generous person . . . can be hurt; and the readiness to forgive is not lightly won: it is part of a character that is subject to great depths of agony."[139] These are insights we desperately need at this time, when so many people are becoming hardened and are losing faith.

If we recognize justice and willingness to forgive as the best human character qualities, we must also recognize them as Godly qualities, and if cruelty and revenge are unworthy human motives they are also unworthy of God. There is a permanent necessity for justice, even in the afterlife, but this does not mean that there is some immovable force ("necessity for punishment") more fundamental than God's will. If God is a loving parent, then correction, guidance, and education are the motives, never punishment as revenge. What kind of selfish parent takes revenge on children? Maybe those children need to be restrained, but never tortured. Certainly there is a need for correction, training, and re-socialization, along with a period of waiting for voluntary repentance, but punishment for its own sake is a wholly unworthy concept; it is

---

[135] Ibid., 64.

[136] Ibid., 71.

[137] Ibid., 72.

[138] Christopher D. Marshall, *Beyond Retribution: A New Testament Vision for Justice, Crime, and Punishment* (Grand Rapids: Eerdmans, 2001) 139. Here and elsewhere he cites Rom 12:21; 1 Thess 5:15; 1 Cor 5:5; 2 Cor 5:6-11; 7:10-11; Gal 6:1; 2 Tim 2:25.

[139] Moule, "Theology of Forgiveness," 65.

motivated either by revenge or by the desire to terrorize others. God, however, is not a Middle Eastern dictator.

Moule's main points are compelling. He shows that the necessary goals of interpersonal reconciliation are education and deterrence, while rejecting any pain infliction that goes beyond these purposes.[140] I would go further than Moule and apply his point to the judicial system: sentencing should be intended to deter that particular criminal, secondarily (if possible) to educate the criminal, finally to bring about some (limited) reparation where this is possible, but not to inflict pain for its own sake. If we really want to understand salvation in terms of God's forgiveness we must repudiate all versions of punitive atonement, since they all assume the necessity of vengeance and punishment (and not for educative or deterrence purposes), with Jesus taking the hit for humanity, and the unsaved being punished for all eternity. There is something morally wrong with that picture. God does not take revenge.

On the contrary, God seeks to save and restore, and rejoices when that is accomplished. This is confirmed in the parable of the Prodigal Son, where the father runs out to greet his wayward son (something extraordinary for a Middle Eastern father) and pours forgiveness on the son without setting any conditions. When the older brother protests against this excessive generosity "his father came out and began to plead with him" (pleading with a son!) and tries to convince him that "we had to celebrate and rejoice."[141] The father's nature is almost over generous; he seeks reconciliation with both sons (*even* the "righteous" one). This brings out an oft-neglected aspect of Jesus' Gospel, that it was an outpouring of joy, like a father finding a long-lost son, or like a person discovering a pearl of great price and selling all he has in order to purchase it.[142]

Human Justice and Atonement Theory

The desire that the perpetrator should be deterred from repeating his wrongs is a worthy one, as is the hope that he should learn why and

---

[140] Plato blends education and deterrence in his concept of justice: "we hope the offender himself and those who observe his punishment, will . . . be brought to loathe injustice" (*Laws*, 934). Quoted in Marshall, *Beyond Retribution*, 104 n. 16.

[141] Luke 15:28, 32.

[142] Joy is one of the "four foci in Jesus' message," along with "compassion; Israel; and kingdom," although the "character of God" underlies them all, according to Klyne Snodgrass, "The Gospel of Jesus," in Markus Bockmuehl and Donald A. Hagner, eds., *The Written Gospel* (Cambridge: Cambridge University Press, 2005) 34. Notions of Jesus as a Cynic sage or political revolutionary cannot account for this joyous emphasis (35).

how these things were wrong. But it is pathological to consider terror and pain to be inherently educative. We law-abiding people are being dishonest when we make this move, pretending that all of our rage is well-intentioned. There are many savage emotions in "civilized" people, and these are almost as big a threat to civilization as are the things criminals do.

Jurisprudence and the imposition of sentences are legitimate for society's self-protection. It has always been a worthy goal of judicial systems to deter repetition of crimes, either by the perpetrator or by other potential perpetrators. Unfortunately, many societies have assumed that cruelty of punishment is the main factor in deterrence, when in fact it has little deterrent effect but is most effective in destroying ethics in society. The United States was right to repudiate and outlaw cruel and unusual punishment. The great Justice Oliver Wendell Holmes recognized that the real deterrent factor was not the *cruelty* of the punishment, but the *certainty* of punishment. Criminals will always take a risk if they know there is a substantial chance of not getting caught, but they *are* deterred if they feel certain they will be caught. The mere *possibility* of being caught and treated cruelly does not deter criminals from taking the risk, because risk is one of the biggest attractions of the game of crime.

Most atonement theories have fatal philosophic flaws, and one of those is mis-assessing what it means to take sin seriously. Atonement theorists frequently say that we are not taking the gravity of sin seriously enough unless we acknowledge that sin must be judged, severely punished, and avenged. This view says that there *must* be vengeance and that the substitutionary death did not remove this unchangeable fact but redirected the punishment. In this view punishment is mandatory, and forgiveness has to await the punishment (perhaps of the innocent). But this is hardly forgiveness; it is *pardon*. Pardon is a legal term; forgiveness is a personal one and is irrelevant in a legal setting. If nothing is superior to this supposed law of punishment, then even God's intention to forgive must find a legal form, such as identifying a substitute victim, since the demands of justice "must" be met (though we would hate to see this kind of "justice" in any human society). To say that punishment is fundamental and unavoidable is to make this law more fundamental than God's own attitude. It means that God is subject to law.[143]

---

[143] Also noted by C. J. den Heyer, *Jesus and the Doctrine of the Atonement: Biblical Notes on a Controversial Topic*, trans. John Bowden (London: SCM, 1998) 132–33.

Most atonement theories say that there *must* be condemnation, conviction, sentencing of sin, and the imposition of that sentence on . . . *someone.* Ironically, this is often equated with justice, despite the diversion of the sentence upon an innocent person, which is never just. If the requirements of justice are irrevocable, this should apply to the execution of the sentence as well.

Atonement theory follows punitive logic 90 percent of the way through, then arbitrarily switches to pardon or acquittal achieved through a legal subterfuge. This is surely dramatic, and it continues to reach the hearts of many people (especially those who have been emotionally damaged and unjustly treated), but it is not logical and does not meet the requirements of either justice or forgiveness. In human affairs real forgiveness seeks no revenge but only repair; this includes an effort to get the wrongdoer to recognize what was wrong about what he did. It may also require the victim to recognize some lesser wrong in what *he* did. It certainly requires a restoration of full and honest communication between the two parties, so that both learn something morally from the experience.

Popular Christian belief thoroughly mixes together the themes of punishment and forgiveness and, unsurprisingly, manifests considerable confusion about both subjects. Supposing that every crime in society must be punished, people have seen this as a fundamental law and have projected this implacable law onto the divine level. Undoubtedly, God has an orderly, thus "lawful," universe, but it is a mistake to think that this is more fundamental than the will of God, that God is *subject* to law, so that God *had* to pour the punishment for human sin onto someone. When punishment is seen as a necessity trumping even the will of God, then monotheism is shattered and forgiveness is betrayed.

Fiddes's Critique

Another worthy attempt to present an orthodox defense of atonement while rejecting anti-moral aberrations of it is that of Paul Fiddes.[144] He is one of those scholars who argue that atonement and justice can be held together, that the "wrath of God" does not imply vindictive or retributive punishment. In effect he seeks to moralize the atonement concept, but I find his critique of Calvin much more convincing than his

---

[144] Paul S. Fiddes, *Past Event and Present Salvation: The Christian Idea of Atonement* (Louisville: Westminster John Knox, 1989).

defense of a blended Pauline, Abelardian, and partially Calvinist atonement idea. He wants simultaneously to preserve the "wrath of God" idea while opposing the notion that God poured his wrath on Christ. So he relies on C. H. Dodd, who argued that the "wrath of God" is not God's personal anger but is a law innate in life itself, whereby sin always reaps a negative consequence:

> To say that Jesus dies under the judgement of God does not mean . . . that God directly *inflicts* some kind of penalty upon him. It is to speak of his complete identification with humankind, and so his experience of the consequences of human sinfulness . . . an enduring of the "wrath" of God.[145]

But this "is not at all . . . an impersonal view of the wrath of God. . . . [God] is involved in the process of natural justice."[146] This seems illogical, but it enables Fiddes to both confirm and deny that God's wrath fell on Christ, *confirming* when he wants to preserve Reformation tradition, *denying* when he wants to preserve a spiritual concept of God. He argues that Calvin recovered the Pauline "insight . . . that Christ endured the wrath and judgement of God," but Calvin "reworked it in terms of criminal law. The result was a theory of 'penal substitution' that is present neither in Paul nor Anselm."[147] It creates a purely artificial kind of atonement that has nothing to do with human repair:

> [In *Inst.* II, 16.3-5] God is propitiating himself. . . . "Propitiation" . . . does not enter the actual sphere of human sin and lack of response to God. . . . Both Calvin's and Anselm's theories . . . portray atonement as a transaction or legal settlement, between God the Father and God the Son in which we are not involved. . . . Atonement is limited to the elect, the ones . . . whose names are written into the legal contract.[148]

Fiddes makes a Dodd-like observation when he says that Paul uses "legal language only to blow the legal system wide open."[149] This overstates and oversimplifies. A legal system is still present in Paul's understanding of our stance in God's court, where a "charge" cannot be brought but only because Christ Jesus "intercedes for us" (Rom 8:33-34). God is still a judge here. The legalistic and penal implications in Paul's

---

[145] Ibid., 91.
[146] Ibid., 93.
[147] Ibid., 98.
[148] Ibid., 70, 99.
[149] Ibid., 86.

metaphors are, indeed, grossly exaggerated and taken much too literally by Calvin (and by the vast majority of Protestants today), but those implications are indeed present in Paul's metaphors. The question, then, becomes: How do we receive Pauline metaphor? Can we reinterpret it in light of our expanding knowledge? For instance, while biblical authors do think of "wrath" as a personal attitude, perhaps we are right to recognize that the "punishing" consequences people encounter are often just the operation of the innate laws of life. We no longer consider every natural disaster an expression of God's wrath; we know more about the operation of physical laws than did people in biblical periods. Can we develop a philosophy that coordinates spiritual reality, moral principle, and physical laws? Are we allowed to interpret the Bible within an updated philosophical framework?

Critiques of Atonement

Some very interesting theological approaches involve a critique of atonement and yet, ironically, some of the theological problems observable in the authors supporting or reshaping atonement recur in different form in these authors' critiques.

5.1A Girard and Friends: The Exposé of Religious Violence

René Girard rejects the notion that the death of Jesus should be considered a sacrifice. Sacrifice is society's technique for sacralizing violence. In fact, says Girard, it is a ritual designed to disguise its systematic violence. Girard's theory is that violence grows out of the common experience of competing for desired goods. Through mimesis (imitation) we learn *what* to desire, and we learn to see others as our rivals for the desired things. This rivalry leads to violence, potentially enough violence to destroy the community. Societies—*all* societies, in fact—develop a technique for focusing their violent energies onto a human victim, a human scapegoat whom the community selects and executes. And this process gets repeated whenever violent tensions build up: "In all human institutions it is necessary to reproduce a reconciliatory murder by means of new victims."[1]

The community then needs to mystify and conceal its violence and so has developed *sacrifice* (a sort of symbolic scapegoat) and *myth* (the grandiose storytelling that implicates God or the gods in the violence). Through a "great coalition of habit and lethargy" people become so

---

[1] René Girard, *Things Hidden Since the Foundation of the World* (London: Athlone, 1987) 53.

wrapped up in distortions that they can "no longer see the lies."[2] The mythology of sacred violence underlies all human religions, Girard says; it attempts to make sacred what is really sordid: ritualized murder performed by the community. But the Gospel exposes "the foundations of all religions in victimage,"[3] for the attack on Jesus was just such a violent scapegoating action by humans.

The sacrificial cult is a pantomime that both inscribes and disguises its predecessor cult: scapegoating. Animal sacrifice, then, simultaneously acts out and covers up the pattern of desire, victim selection, and communal violence. This is an interesting analysis, but it is too simple. It is hardly plausible that all societies developed the exact same rage-focusing procedure and that it is not even worth mentioning the other rage-focusing techniques that have been developed: palaver and compromise, adjudication, athletics, dramatized violence and storytelling, internalized violence and shamanic journeys, war against other communities. Further, Girard's theory would require that some vestiges of social rage would still be visible in animal sacrifice, but just the opposite is true. From Greece to Iran to Israel there is no sign of *rage* being focused on the victim; in fact, humanitarian swiftness of execution is the rule, which is *not* true about expulsion rituals. Even the Jewish scapegoat ritual involved the pouring of abuse onto the victim. Nothing like this is seen in Jewish sacrifice. The leap from scapegoat to sacrifice is one of several weak links in Girardian theory.

In fact, the "sacred" involves many intuitions, hopes, symbols, valuations, codes, systems, and mental games. Girard has done an immense service by showing that violence is *one* of the things that is drawn into the sacred and treated with awe. But by no means is violence the single underlying subject matter of the "sacred." The notion that scapegoating is the sole content of the sacred and the primary basis of all cultures and myths is both incredible and hyperpessimistic. And yet Girard has touched on some powerful truth, or his theory would not have such interpretive power.

The theory can usefully be brought to bear on stories of rivalry and violence (often between brothers) and divine violence in OT narratives[4]

[2] Raymund Schwager, *Jesus in the Drama of Salvation: Toward a Biblical Doctrine of Redemption*, trans. James G. Williams and Paul Haddon (New York: Crossroad, 1999) 91.

[3] Girard, *Things Hidden*, 184.

[4] James G. Williams, *The Bible, Violence, and the Sacred: Liberation from the Myth of Sanctioned Violence* (San Francisco: HarperSanFrancisco, 1991) 50–58, 117–37; Raymund Schwager, *Must There Be Scapegoats? Violence and Redemption in the Bible* (New York: Crossroad, 2000) 47–75.

and in the Psalms,[5] and on the seriousness of prophetic resistance to sacrificial violence.[6] It is within the OT that we see the beginning of the work of exposing the pattern of violence. For instance, the Tenth Commandment prohibits envy, which is what leads to theft and murder and all the other crimes. The prophets began to expose the violent scapegoat mechanism, but they faltered because they could not escape from the general tendency to make God the source of everything, good and evil. Walter Wink restates Girard's and Schwager's view of "the Hebrew Bible as a long and laborious exodus out of the world of violence, an exodus plagued by repeated reversals."[7]

It is only in the gospels that the mob's violence is exposed as dishonest, not really sacred. It is the mob that is guilty; the victim is innocent.[8] The gospels denounce the crime rather than making it a sacred ritual event, nor did Jesus take on "sacred" blame, as many victims do. Jesus' death is not a sacrifice but an *exposé* of sacrifice and of the lying mythology that tries to implicate God in the selection of victims. God is not the source of human violence. Atonement theories that have God requiring a sacrifice perpetuate the old view that "the Father of Jesus is still a God of violence, despite what Jesus explicitly says. Indeed he comes to be the God of unequalled violence . . . envisag[ing] taking revenge upon the whole of mankind for a death that he both required and anticipated."[9]

Girard points out the contradiction in simultaneously blaming God and blaming human beings for the death of Jesus. He argues that the gospels do not teach sacrificial soteriology but, rather, expose sacrificial violence and religious hypocrisy: "The Gospels only speak of *sacrifices* in order to reject them. . . . Jesus counters the ritualism of the Pharisees with an anti-sacrificial quotation from Hosea. . . . There is nothing in the Gospels to suggest that the death of Jesus is a sacrifice."[10]

Sometimes one or another evangelist fails to comprehend this, falling back into a sacrificial (violent) interpretation, Girard says. For instance, at the end of the parable of the tenants Mark and Luke have Jesus saying that God would destroy the wicked tenants, but Matthew correctly retains

[5] Schwager, *Must There Be Scapegoats?* 92–110.

[6] Williams, *Bible, Violence, and the Sacred*, 148–61; Schwager, *Must There Be Scapegoats?* 82–91.

[7] Walter Wink, *The Powers That Be: Theology for a New Millennium* (New York: Doubleday, 1998) 84.

[8] René Girard, *I See Satan Fall Like Lightning*, trans. James G. Williams (Maryknoll, NY: Orbis, 2001) 21–22, 35–36.

[9] Girard, *Things Hidden*, 213.

[10] Ibid., 180.

the dialogue in which Jesus asks the crowd what would happen to those tenants, and *they* speak of violent punishment, which people "imprisoned within the sacrificial vision" can hardly help doing. But Matthew could not see Jesus himself saying that.[11] Similarly, the violent apocalyptic sayings in the gospels should not be attributed to the real Jesus;[12] we need to use historical critical tools to try to recover the historical Jesus.

> If we keep to the passages that relate specifically to the Father of Jesus, we can easily see they contain nothing which would justify attributing the least amount of violence to the deity. . . . [T]he immemorial and unconscious practice of making the deity responsible for all the evils that can afflict humanity is thus explicitly repudiated.[13]

Unfortunately, Girard comes close to resuscitating the violent atonement idea he all but destroyed when he speaks of God anticipating that Satan would bring about violence against Jesus, that God even *planned* to make use of that violence to expose the "scapegoat mechanism" in human society.[14] Girard is not very clear on whether he is actually reviving a form of the old theory of the Son being predestined to be killed, but it certainly comes dangerously close to reestablishing scapegoating as a divine mechanism and evil personalities as agents of God's will—all the distorted ideas he had set out to overturn! For Girardian theory to work, God needs to reject *all* scapegoating. Using it once is once too often. Of course, there is a difference between *intending* something to happen and merely *anticipating* it and making it work for good. This is a crucial distinction and one that needs to be made crystal clear if Girard's theory is to work. There is a world of difference between a God-caused death and a God-anticipated death.

As an anthropological theory, the fatal flaw in Girard's proposal is the reductionist insistence that all culture and religion are founded on one thing, the scapegoating mechanism. Even if it could be shown that there is such a mechanism in societies around the world, that would only prove its existence, not its primacy in social formation. In fact, there are numerous (but less thrilling) reasons for the formation of human societies: the advantages of coordinating efforts at securing food, shelter, and defense. In the realm of abstraction and symbolic thought there are numerous

---

[11] Ibid., 187–88.
[12] Ibid., 203–04, 272.
[13] Ibid., 182–83.
[14] Girard, *I See Satan*, 151–52.

activities that have nothing to do with scapegoating but much to do with perception of social and natural order, memorialization of relationships, and conceptualization of deities and spirits. It may be that scapegoating needs to take its place among many other conceptual patterns that can be seen in religions, but its place is not the foundation stone. All society would be irredeemably evil if that were the case; the mere *exposé* of violence would not be enough to change those whose whole mentality is shaped by millennia of lies and violence.

If there is no other basis to human religion than violence and dissembling, then humanity is doomed. Nothing but violence and lies would *ever* rule. If human beings around the world and in their nonbiblical religions had not learned anything about justice, honesty, compassion, reciprocity, compromise, repentance, repair, afterlife, spirituality, or perfection of motivation, how could the Gentiles ever be attracted to the gospel or know how to take in its insights? And if the Bible revealed a process of gradual ethical progress and insight into the scapegoat mechanism, does not this make *progress* (not scapegoating) the real—long-term—foundation of society? Both religion and society are much more complicated than Girardian theory has been able to articulate.

Nevertheless, there is no denying (at least from *this* quarter) that Girard has helped expose and partially explain the violence of even (or especially?) the most moralistic religious institutions, followed by the concealment and mythologizing that really does happen in human religions, not least of all in Christianity. No other religion has so hypocritically betrayed the principles of its founder, especially during the violent persecutions of the thirteenth to seventeenth centuries, but not restricted to that period by any means.

5.1B Ideologies of Blame and Revenge

Girard's theory does offer some assistance in our effort to comprehend a phenomenon that seems to be growing more severe and widespread with time: political scapegoating. Whether taking place in highly sophisticated industrialized societies (Germany), societies making an ungainly transition from agriculture to industry (Russia), or preindustrial societies (Rwanda), political scapegoating can become all-consuming in whole societies. There is an ugly human inclination to focus blame and to take revenge. There is no difference in method, only in details, between Hutu leaders vilifying the Tutsi, Hitler's systematic blaming of the Jews for Germany's defeat in World War I, and Russian Socialists' discussion of which groups were to be blamed and punished ("whom shall we beat?"). Radical Islam's blaming of "Zionism" for every problem in Islamic societies matches these other ideologies in simplistic analysis and ferocious feeling.

The ideology that has been particularly "successful" at the blame game over the last century is Marxism. Because it does have some actual explanatory power and because it purports to be for the good of all the "exploited classes" it was a particularly effective response to exploitation in the Industrial Revolution. It took advantage of social breakdown during World War I, stimulated labor and political unrest and so helped lead to World War II, and drove a prolonged and ugly competition between superpowers that was hardly a "cold" war for those who were burned in it.

Marxism provided the theoretical basis for much of the social analysis and attempted remediation in the last forty years. Marxist thinking took a strategic turn in the 1960s, reinventing itself in various guises as liberationist movements directed against particular groups: "white society," men ("all men are rapists"), and the current favorite—white males. The possibility that white males may also be oppressed is dogmatically denied. Once the oppressor class has been identified, it must be attacked without restraint. The enemy of the people has been identified; you know what to do.

Marxian thinking is so widespread that it no longer needs to be backed up with complicated class analysis or directed by a Leninist party. Any intellectual can become a new Lenin. Everyone knows how to practice Marxian scapegoating: simply identify the class to be blamed, make simplistic and sweeping condemnations, and see if concessions start flowing from the accused. Marxian discourse is emotionally satisfying and politically effective.

Theologians should take closer notice of the spirit of Marxism but not embrace it. What motivates Marxism is not the humanitarianism it claims but the enticing image of mob revolt and justified violence. Marxism's greatest appeal is its promise of justice through revenge. It is Messianic and apocalyptic in its call for redemptive violence. It is quasi-religious in promoting its self-righteous missionary violence. It preserves some of the worst aspects of nonprogressive religion.

Marxian analysis acts along Girardian scapegoating lines, except that the chosen scapegoat will be a class or a group rather than an individual. But the pattern of selection, vilification, blame, and unrestrained violence is even uglier than what Girard describes. It would create a new society "buil[t] by bloodshed" (Hab 2:12). But this does not release social pressure, as Girard theorizes; it is more crude and less therapeutic than that. Violent political scapegoating *generates* rather than reduces violence. Girardian theory needs to be revised so as to recognize the pathology of political scapegoating.

It may be that political scapegoating has always been the means by which hierarchical societies eject guilt feelings: "the 'guilt' intrinsic to hierarchical order (the only kind of 'organizational' order we have ever known) calls correspondingly for 'redemption' through *victimage*."[15] Whether or not Girardians decide to accept this, they need to interact more with other approaches and observe recent political history more closely.

If we are to cease being swept away by our own violent tendencies we must combine our knowledge of religion, psychology, and politics and clear away our violent delusions. We should be ready now to recognize Marxism as an ideology of revenge and to repudiate it utterly. Marxism has done nothing to reverse the patterns of land loss, debt slavery, and dependency faced by the lower middle class and the poor; its gospel of hate has only made the problems of oppression and violence worse. It has now been eclipsed, in the war against culture, by radical Islam.

5.2A Nelson-Pallmeyer: Compassion, Not Atonement

In lieu of discussing the many other critics of atonement whose writings are of interest, I now deal with that critic whose writing has stimulated me to develop the beginning of a philosophical approach to religious progress.

Jack Nelson-Pallmeyer departs significantly from all the defenders of atonement and also from Girard. He rejects the theology of violence, even when it is found in the Bible. Nelson-Pallmeyer is the most consistent and focused spokesman for a certain moral viewpoint, one that rejects all violent images of God and utterly repudiates the idea that Jesus taught that God would be violent. He is to be commended for this, but his interpretation is lacking in some essential aspects, which I will discuss.

After reviewing many stories of "God's redemptive violence"[16] against all Egyptian firstborn children, against all "the inhabitants of the land"[17]

---

[15] Kenneth Burke, *Permanence and Change: An Anatomy of Purpose*, rev. ed. (Los Altos, CA: Hermes, 1954) 284.

[16] Jack Nelson-Pallmeyer, *Jesus Against Christianity: Reclaiming the Missing Jesus* (Harrisburg: Trinity Press International, 2001) 55.

[17] Ibid., 39.

between the Mediterranean and the Euphrates (Exod 23:31), against every Midianite male and nonvirginal woman (Num 31:17-18),[18] and against forty-two children who dared to taunt a prophet by saying "go away, baldhead" (2 Kgs 2:23-24),[19] Nelson-Pallmeyer has to conclude that "much of the Bible" says that "God is . . . vile, hateful, and murderous," taking "control of the Promised Land through genocide."[20] Nor is the problem solved by assigning all difficulties to the OT; a number of NT books invest hope in future apocalyptic violence. Further, "We must choose between competing portraits of Jesus and incompatible images of God" (page 293). If we take Jesus' own teachings seriously we must reject the concept of a tempestuous and violent God. For Jesus, "God is not violent and God's power is not coercive" (page 305); "God's power is invitational" (289).

He points out that, too often, "the nonviolence of Jesus . . . is acknowledged but ignored" (216). Peace activists take it seriously, but they often buy into the theology of divine retribution. For instance, "[Richard] Horsley roots the nonviolence of Jesus in the apocalyptic violence of God" (217). But Jesus means his nonviolence to be a revelation of God's way (Matt 5:43-48). He means to destroy violent ideation itself: "Jesus shatters the mythology of redemptive violence" (88). It is illogical to say that "God who is nonviolent used human projections of a violent God for good" (222), an error into which some important scholars fall, such as Horsley and even Walter Wink at some points.[21]

Nelson-Pallmeyer sees a dark foundation to atonement and the connections it calls for, such as the idea that Christ's death functioned like the blood of the Passover, enabling God to pass over the sins of Christians: Although "wrap[ped] in the language of love, the unspoken implication is that God's wrath could only be appeased through the blood sacrifice of a divine son" (155). Atonement theories are driven by "pathological portraits of God" (155). Nelson-Pallmeyer's consistent word on the subject is that "Jesus was not sent by God to die in order to appease a violent deity. . . . His death was not an atoning sacrifice or a way of bringing a scapegoat mechanism to light" (225).

---

[18] Ibid., 32.

[19] Ibid., 25–26.

[20] Ibid., 64, 311.

[21] Ibid., 222–24, citing Wink's defense of a "necessary" jealousy and violence and of God using the death of Jesus to expose the scapegoat mechanism (Wink, *The Powers That Be*, 85–89).

5.2B The Slide into Anti-Biblicism

But Nelson-Pallmeyer goes much further than this. The biblical evangelists betray, more than they proclaim, Jesus' message: "The Gospel writers betray Jesus when they recast oppressive actors in the domination system as God-figures in the retelling of Jesus' parables" (277). Matthew is the worst: he creates violent God-figures who "consistently send people to the torturers . . . entirely at odds with the images of God that guided Jesus" (293).

It should not be hard to concede that "flawed human beings wrote the Bible" (176), but Nelson-Pallmeyer goes far beyond that: "vile and violent portrayals overwhelm positive images of God within the Bible" (138) and, in fact, "Jesus is essentially missing from Christianity" (153). Of course, these conclusions would call for much more than a mere "challeng[ing of] scriptural authority" (65)! They would demand a complete rejection of the Bible, but he holds back from expressing what seems to be the logical outcome of his own reasoning.

At least in some of his observations the Bible is not a factor for good. Nelson-Pallmeyer notes that many atheists or agnostics are "at least as ethical" as many Christians and Muslims, who are compassionate *"in spite of much of what is in their 'sacred' texts."*[22] Why does he never come out and say that these texts should be simply rejected? I consider three possible reasons: (1) the occasional truth he sees in the Bible is enough to preclude his rejecting it; but this is a weak possibility, since positive images are "overwhelmed" by vile ones; (2) saying "reject the Bible altogether" would alienate a portion of his audience, so he pulls back from this conclusion for purely tactical reasons; (3) he has not rejected the Bible, but he *has* rejected the concept of sacred and infallible Scriptures. He uses the Bible because he finds parts of it that are truthful; he simply no longer treats the collection as sacred. The third choice clearly has the most explanatory power as regards Nelson-Pallmeyer's position, and it does not require us to see him as unreasonable.

Advantages to Nelson-Pallmeyer's analysis are ethical consistency, intellectual integrity, and a strong defense of Jesus' teaching of "God's noncoercive, nonviolent power."[23] Disadvantages are that his views would logically call for a rejection of the concept of Scripture, or of any special status for the Bible. He never says what would replace the Bible

---

[22] Jack Nelson-Pallmeyer, *Is Religion Killing Us? Violence in the Bible and the Quran* (Harrisburg: Trinity Press International, 2003) 132.

[23] Nelson-Pallmeyer, *Jesus Against Christianity,* 320.

for the church if it were suddenly regarded as nothing more than human theology, full of vile misrepresentations. Although he never says, "the Bible is nothing special and the church should stop regarding it as such," his logic leads that way, and he never gives a good reason for *not* saying this. In my view the reason for this breakdown in Nelson-Pallmeyer's analysis is his failure to account for the changing views of God in the Bible and to perceive the progress in religious conceptualization that takes place within the Bible, which is a record of gradual human absorption of and interpretation of revelation received from God. We need to study the human reception of revelation.

Nelson-Pallmeyer's critique of the biblical past is implicitly evolutional, yet he fails to articulate an evolutionary concept. His attacks on biblical rhetoric are not accompanied by adequate explanation, thus leaving the impression that the Bible does more harm than good. His condemnatory powers exceed his explanatory ones: he is a prophet, himself! But a prophet now must be a philosopher as well. Repudiating biblical rhetoric without accounting for it is destructive. No repudiation without explanation!

Nelson-Pallmeyer does seem to recognize that his moral umbrage at certain Bible passages is itself an ethical by-product of having read and taken to heart *other* Bible passages, but he does not draw a hermeneutical conclusion from this: that the Bible is its own best critic; that the Bible shows stages of progressive ethical development. A hermeneutic of religious progress would enable us to understand, not condemn, the earlier phases of development. The first step, though, is to recognize what the literature is meant to accomplish.

Recognizing Literary Genres in the Bible

To attack every violent image of God as bad dogma is to take an overly dogmatic approach. It is dogmatic to treat every biblical statement as a dogma. Further, it is a genre mistake. In the genre of prophetic rhetoric, dramatic flair and a judgmental tone were *recognized* and *expected*. The Bible is not a long string of dogmatic statements. Much of the Bible is narrative and needs to be read as *story*, with moral lessons appropriated through one's emotional participation in the story. Different characters will utter different truths or truisms, but the truth of the whole is often greater than the truth uttered by any one character. Prophetic oracle, on the other hand, is a completely different genre. Prophetic oracle is both poetic and political, both abstract and concrete, both beautiful and harsh; it participates in poetic imagination and public debate—a fiery debate, no doubt, wherein exaggeration and intensity are recognized tools of the trade. Attacking prophetic statements as wrong dogmas is overly dogmatic and insufficiently attuned to the literary genre. Without literary imagination one cannot follow either a story or an oracle. Further, one will fail to notice sarcasm (as in Isaiah), or even mockery of the genre (as in Jonah).

Many of the theological views Nelson-Pallmeyer condemns were an advance on an older view. The Bible does show God's gradually unfolding plan. Jesus did not feel the need to attack the Bible, though he did build on certain favorite passages (Pss 51 and 110; Hos 6:6; Isa 61). Jesus is not the first person to have a "canon within the canon," to make certain passages, certain insights controlling. And what he leaves out is significant. As Nelson-Pallmeyer points out, when Jesus uses Isaiah 61 to announce his teaching and healing ministry he leaves out "the day of vengeance" from 61:2.[24]

If biblical authors are "both insightful and fallible and thus capable of both revealing and distorting God,"[25] this cries out for a systematic framework for evaluating biblical texts, something more than simply condemning every judgmental image. A better approach would be to appreciate the genre and study the flow of rhetoric and ideas within which a biblical text occurs so as to assess its contribution to the course of religious evolution. One will have to conclude that some statements were cruel and nonprogressive even for their time, such as the story of bears attacking children who teased a prophet (a story used to threaten children?). But one will likely find that some of the judgmental and threatening passages were philosophically advanced for their time. When Isaiah calls for Judah to defend orphans and widows (1:17), and threatens invasion if it abandons that ethic (1:20), Nelson-Pallmeyer sees only a threat that widows and orphans will be crushed,[26] but that is exactly what Isaiah's warning is meant to *prevent*. However, it cannot be prevented, the prophet insists, unless Israel is loyal to covenant ethics.

The threats were not imaginary; the danger of Assyrian invasion was very real. Jesus uttered warnings as severe as those of Isaiah, Hosea, and Jeremiah: the nation will be punished if it goes on rebelling against God—and the nation *was* punished (or something that could be so interpreted) in the wars of 720 B.C.E., 587 B.C.E., and 70 C.E. We should see beyond the sometimes-offensive rhetoric to the noble purpose behind

---

[24] Luke 4:18-19; Nelson-Pallmeyer, *Jesus Against Christianity*, 321.

[25] Nelson-Pallmeyer, *Is Religion Killing Us?* 134.

[26] Nelson-Pallmeyer, *Jesus Against Christianity*, 103.

the warning. The judgmental rhetoric was intended to awaken the people and turn them away from making choices that would lead the nation to doom by undermining the only thing that gave Israel and Judah a unique role in the world.

The Monotheist Hermeneutic

Occasionally Nelson-Pallmeyer's arguments are strangely unimaginative. He looks at the two narratives threaded together in Genesis, using the different names Yahweh and Elohim, and says "one god + one god = one God is bad math" (70). "We cannot . . . dismiss the problem of two gods by saying that the two creation stories are about the same God known by two different names" (67)—but the entire Jewish and Christian traditions have said exactly that. They bring a monotheistic understanding to the text; in fact, they *impose* a monotheistic hermeneutic on the text. It is the imposition of this overarching hermeneutic upon a group of texts that enables a sacred collection to develop and endure. Nelson-Pallmeyer may be correct in saying that the two creation texts originally came from two different communities (or two different subregions within the Israelite community), and almost everyone would accept his statement that they were written by two different authors, but that does not stop the flow of hermeneutical history. The embedding of these texts in a bigger text is more important than either passage by itself. A large part of the perceived meaning of these texts derives from their having been collected into a book (Genesis) and a supercollection (the Bible). By placing these works in the Bible, the community said, "these all speak of the one God; we believe in a creator God." The canonical process *matters*. It may indeed result in suppression of difficulties and contradictions in the texts, but the emergence of a dominant spiritualizing hermeneutic (monotheism) necessitated this suppression. (It is "spiritualizing" in that it imposes a spiritual interpretation on a primitive text and in the sense that it reflects progress toward more universalizing, and less tribalistic, loyalties and understandings.)

The Bible is a many-layered painting. The lower layers of paint have been partly covered by more recent layers. Scholarship peels back the layers, examines the underlying pigments, notices that certain figures have been altered, takes note of the different painting styles, and tries to understand what motivated the changes.

Many of the older texts testify to a belief that other nations had other gods, but the monotheistic hermeneutic reinterprets and rejects that. The voice of Second Isaiah saying that there is only one God is louder than the voice of any text that speaks of Chemosh for the Moabites and Dagon for the Philistines. Isaiah mocks these as human fabrications. As we come forward in time, all serious Jews and Christians are monotheists.

Religious and Philosophic Progress

If I persist in criticizing Nelson-Pallmeyer it is because I consider his insight clear enough and his work important enough to treat him as a major thinker on this subject. I also think his failure to see progressive revelation (or human response to progressive revelation) in the Bible is a common failing, and one that cries out for correction. Nelson-Pallmeyer says that I am trying to "save biblical authority,"[27] but I am not arguing for biblical infallibility or promoting a sacred status, beyond criticism, for the Bible. I *am* arguing for a recognition of philosophic and ethical progress within the Bible. This is because the Bible contains genuine divine revelation, though mediated through humans. The NT is a human response to, and interpretation of, the revelation of the life of the Son of Man and Son of God. But the Bible also contains superstition (testing a woman's fidelity by making her drink a concoction of sweepings from the temple floor, Num 5:12-13, 17-31), anger (many psalms), even geno-cide (Num 31:17), things that should not be treated as anything other than human. These things would not be there if the Bible were directly authored by God. And yet there has been divine guidance of the biblical process; the diamonds in the Bible are not there by accident. There is something divine, as well as much that is human, in the Bible. We need to revise our understanding of it, though. God reveals truth and good-ness to us but also allows us to thoroughly humanize, adapt, interpret, and even degrade what has been revealed. Therefore we must continu-ally endeavor to clear away corruption wherever it occurs, even within the pages of the Bible.

But we should do this within the context of a farsighted understand-ing of how ethical progress takes place. Nelson-Pallmeyer is too rigid in offering only two choices, which he italicizes to heighten the sharpness of the choice: "*either God is a pathological killer because the Bible says so, or the Bible is sometimes wrong about God*" (63). Why must we accept such a narrow choice? There is a third choice: that the understanding of God was evolving within the biblical periods, and we see these stages of

---

[27] Nelson-Pallmeyer, personal e-mail communication.

evolution (and sometimes of regression) in the pages of the Bible. Even the judgmental images of God are *legitimate* stages in the evolution of the God-concept. Ideas of God must be assessed with due consideration of the social, philosophical, and ideational levels of the original author and readers. One cannot expect a sixth-century B.C.E. person to advocate ecofeminism and fair-trade coffee beans. The insights that were necessary and appropriate for First Isaiah's time were that God is One, God is just, and human behavior will be rewarded or punished on the basis of its justice or lack of justice. That was an advance, in its time. Failure to recognize this leads to failure to respect and understand the prophets. They *needed* an image of the judgment of God, just as we now need images of the peace of God. The stage where there must be sharp differentiation between right and wrong, with recognition that wrong will be judged, is an earlier stage than the one that we are at now—or are *trying* to be at—in which different races, nationalities, and religions need to coexist peacefully. But the transition to peaceful coexistence will be impossible if we lose sight of earlier truths about right and wrong.

We no longer believe (at least, Nelson-Pallmeyer and I do not believe) that God punishes nations by sending earthquakes (Amos 9:5 LXX: "he takes hold of the land and causes it to shake"), but I think we should grant Amos the right to use that primitive idea as a way of grabbing the people's attention and imparting something of higher and nobler truth, the motivation toward a justice-dominated society. In Amos 5:10-17, 24-27 we see that the threats grow out of the tragic fact of corruption in the city gate (where judicial cases were heard), unfair economic practice, and a choosing of ritual over justice. It is not enough to just advocate right and condemn wrong. Amos and the other prophets, including the great prophets of Iran (Zarathushtra), China (Confucius), and India (Buddha) all found it necessary to establish that one does not get away with wrongdoing. Whether one stresses the afterlife (Zarathushtra, Buddha) or this life (Amos, Confucius), it is necessary to know that wrong will be punished. Nor should we analyze this strictly from the standpoint of parental psychology, as though this were nothing more than the voice of a scolding parent. Something much deeper and more permanent is at stake here, a law to which parents, also, are subject.

We now have a more advanced scientific viewpoint than any of the biblical authors possessed. In prescientific ages, when God was blamed for everything that happened, tragedies were explained as punishments. With better scientific and philosophic tools, we no longer do that. It is to be hoped that we will also assess ancient texts in light of ancient worldviews and literary genres, with an ability to recognize philosophical and ethical progress where it exists.

Along with this goes the ability to discern regression, which temporarily derails the advance of truth. Cultic atonement is such a regressive idea. The ancient idea of God as a raging fire, subject to harsh laws of retribution, undermines the teaching of the loving and parental watchful care of God. Atonement is a millstone around the neck of Christianity, preventing further advances in psychological health and family ethics. I see only three main options for handling atonement theology: primitivizing, spiritualizing, or rejecting. One must either affirm a violent God concept, explain it away allegorically, or openly reject it as a misconception. The third option means admitting that such outmoded ideas are present in our Bible. To be a mature Christian now means to be a Bible critic. Because of scientific and social advances, Christianity now carries a heavier intellectual demand than ever before. Can we develop reflective approaches to the Bible and avoid simplistic approaches of either the left or the right (*The Da Vinci Code* or the *Left Behind* series)? There is no other responsible alternative. We must love God with all our *minds* as well as with our hearts and souls.

The recognition that wrongdoing leads to harsh consequences is necessary in the evolution of religion. I will call this the truth of Judgment. Just as children make every newly-learned lesson all-consuming, humanity overdeveloped its conceptualization of Judgment, generating ideas of savage punishment and divine wrath that are simply implausible for those who have heard and embraced the *next* great truth-revelation: the truth of Parental Love.

When religions fail to make progress, they become obsessed with some truth, often the truth of Judgment. This truth was twisted out of recognition when religious ideology generated pious murderers, from the priest Phinehas to the Inquisitor Torquemada to the puritan Oliver Cromwell to the ayatollahs in Iran. These deformations of "righteousness" show how easy it is to marry our piety to our narcissism and to paint our defensiveness as heroism. The truth of Judgment cannot operate alone; if the truth of Loving-kindness is beyond its reach, it needs, at least, to join the truth of Mercy.

But the truth of Judgment does make a real advance when it removes retribution from human hands. Deferral of retribution to God corresponds to that healthy psychological response called sublimation. Attribution of violence to God is healthy when it means violence is removed as an option for humans, even though such attribution will create theological problems for later generations. In the same way the psychological adaptations of adolescence create problems for adulthood. Every phase that is functional for a while becomes nonfunctional when new advances are needed. Yet there are things from each previous stage that need to be retained.

We see many phases of such advancing within the pages of the Bible. The priests (the "P" author) tried to suppress the anthropomorphism of the earlier stage, setting up a ritual technology for cleansing the nation; the prophets attacked that ritual system when they saw it becoming a hypocritical cover for evil behavior; Jesus speaks like a prophet when he says the Pharisees have been concerned with "dill, and cummin, and have neglected the weightier matters of the law: justice and mercy and faith" (Matt 23:23). A prophet has to attack "greed and self-indulgence" (Matt 23:25) in order to defend justice and mercy. Instead of ritual cleanness, a prophet demands: "first clean the inside" (v. 26). His ethical imperative is the same as Hosea's: "if you had known what this means, 'I desire mercy and not sacrifice,' you would not have condemned the guiltless" (Matt 12:7; cf. Hos 6:6). Jesus expresses the truth of Judgment *and* the truth of Mercy.

The great theologian Gregory of Nazianzus gives one of the clearest explanations of the necessity for religious conceptual growth. Gregory wrote:

> The Old Testament proclaimed the Father openly, and the Son more obscurely. The New manifested the Son, and suggested the Deity of the Holy Spirit. Now the Spirit Himself dwells among us. . . . For it was not safe, when the Godhead of the Father was not yet acknowledged, plainly to proclaim the Son; nor when that of the Son was not yet received to burden us . . . with the Holy Ghost . . . [B]y gradual additions . . . and progress from glory to glory, the Light of the Trinity might shine upon the more illuminated. [28]
>
> You see lights breaking upon us gradually; and the order of Theology, which it is better for us to keep, neither proclaiming things too suddenly, nor yet keeping them hidden to the end. [29]

Growing from Our Heritage

If the light of God (Trinity) issues progressive revelation designed to illuminate humanity, this fact needs to shape our understanding of the evolution of religion. It is certainly a tragic mistake to offer only a non-

---

[28] Fifth Theological Oration: "On the Holy Spirit" 26; in NPNF 2, 7:326.
[29] "On the Holy Spirit" 27, NPNF 2, 7:326.

evolutionary choice, forcing us either to be stuck in the past or to repudiate the past. We would do better to remember that humans have to grow
out of the past in two senses: we do need to grow up and leave behind
certain concepts of the past, but we also shape our present from the raw
materials of our past, thus benefiting from the past. So we grow *from* as
well as grow *away from* the past.

We need both sides of this growth process, and Second Isaiah can
provide the slogan for both sides: "Look to the rock from which you
were hewn, and to the quarry from which you were dug" (51:1)—*retain*
your heritage, your covenant with God. But also recognize that "new
things I now declare. . . . Behold, I am doing a new thing; now it springs
forth, do you not perceive it?" (42:9; 43:19 RSV)—the covenant has been
redefined; have you understood it? Second Isaiah and Jeremiah made a
start at redefining the covenant. Jesus expands on their concept of heart-
felt loyalty as the real basis of the covenant relationship with God.[30] Each
covenant grows out of the previous one, or rather, out of the best reinterpretation of the previous one. But this does not mean rejection of the
monotheistic heritage; we grow from that heritage. We need to recognize
the necessity of gradual moral progress, spiritual evolution. The era of
Judgment needs to be absorbed by the emerging era of Parental Love.

Without a perspective of revelational evolution the violence in the
Bible is intolerable, and one must either take on a willful blindness to
the ugliness of violence or else slide toward a rejection of the Bible. But
with a concept of revelation and evolution one can begin to see the action
of God on the evolving concepts of the biblical authors, gradually pre-
paring the Jews for the arrival of the Messiah who would try to "open
. . . the scriptures to us" (Luke 24:32).

[30] On a new covenant written on peoples' hearts see Jer 24:7; 29:13; 31:31-34; 32:39-40.
All humankind will see it: Isa 40:5; 42:6; 49:6; 51:4. On the idea of a new spirit, a covenant
of the spirit, or a law written on the mind see Isa 11:2-5; 42:1; 44:3; 59:21; 61:1; Ezek 37:26;
36:26; 39:29; 2 Cor 3:3-6; John 3:34; Heb 10:16.

A Theory of Revelation and Evolution

6.1 The Effect of Revelation

Revelation itself is not evolutionary in origin, but the *effects* of revelation are. The human retelling of the encounter, the discussion and attempted comprehension of the revelatory teachings, the human grasp of values and comprehension of essential meanings—all these are evolutionary. They are part of human discussion, philosophy, institution formation, and liturgy. They become subject to recognizable patterns of psychology, sociology, and change over time.[1] We can study the human end of the encounter with revelation. The wind blows where it wills, and we hear the sound of it, but we know not whence it comes or where it goes (John 3:8). We see the wind's effect but cannot see the wind, though its effects are highly suggestive.

If revelation enters the human world even for a moment, the world is forever changed. The world continues to function according to the rules of nature, but something has been altered. The aftereffects of divine visitation become part of the human system, and the course of evolution is subtly shifted. An idea like faith or forgiveness, previously peripheral, becomes central. Everything still obeys the laws of evolution, but evolution itself has been redirected ("everything has become new!" 2 Cor 5:17). A leavening from heaven has been added to our earthly lump, and if we knead it into the evolutionary dough, the bread will rise.

---

[1] This is true although the greatest weakness of social theory has been its "failure to deal with change" (Hugh Dalziel Duncan, *Symbols and Social Theory* [New York: Oxford University Press, 1969] 139).

As soon as revelation is received by humans, it becomes evolutionary, human, fallible—but it can still be very good. Everything that is touched by humans is fallible. Further, the revelatory message is *shaped* by the emotions, the revulsions, the hopes, the viewpoints of the humans who receive it: "The spirits of prophets are subject to the prophets" (1 Cor 14:32).

A theory of revelational evolution can help account for continuity and discontinuity in religious thought over time. Sometimes revelation takes issue with something in the religious heritage and initiates a hermeneutic of rejection. Thus in Israelite religion there is both a perpetuation of and a ridiculing of sacrifice. Israelite argues with Israelite over this issue. In Christianity there has been a wide diversity of interpretations of sacrificial and atonement imagery from the very beginning, and this must continue. We must ask whether our response to ancient religious ideas is progressive or not, whether we are "like the master of a household who brings out of his treasure what is new and what is old" (Matt 13:52) or whether "for the sake of your tradition, you make void the word of God" (Matt 15:6).

Revelation always builds on the evolutionary results of prior revelation. Whenever Jesus articulated a higher stage of religious insight he built on prior traditions, comparing himself to Solomon, saying "keep the commandments" and "what is written in the law?"[2]—but he also took issue with the tradition or heightened its moral intensity by contrasting his teachings with some maxims of the Law, saying "you have heard . . . but I say" (Matt 5:21-22, 27-28, 31-34, 38-39), and refusing to enact a (supposedly) Mosaic instruction.[3] He could use the tradition against the tradition, as when he challenged the habit of calling the Messiah the son of David and reminded people of instances in which the Law's rules were bent.[4] Nevertheless, Jesus built his message on the Hebrew Scriptures. In fact, his sayings were only comprehensible if one activated the truth of the prior stage. Without vigorous loyalty to the insight one has, one does not get the new insight. One must be honestly loyal at one's current stage of development before taking the next step.

Every revelation builds on the evolutionary response to prior revelation. When Jesus meets Nathanael he sees just that honesty ("an Israelite in whom there is no deceit!" John 1:47), vigorous enough to question

---

[2] Matt 12:42; 19:17; Luke 10:26.
[3] John 8:5-11.
[4] Mark 12:35-37; Matt 12:2-8; John 7:23.

who this so-called Messiah might be (1:46). Matching Jesus' quick insight, Nathanael quickly sees the divinity of Jesus and affirms it ("you are the Son of God," 1:49). Jesus promptly makes a stunning revelation to Nathanael about the levels within the heavenly and angelic hierarchy: "you will see heaven opened and the angels of God ascending and descending upon the Son of Man" (1:51). God responds to human readiness with an abundance of revelation. It is an acted-out fulfillment of the prophetic promise, "When you search for me, you will find me; if you seek me with all your heart, I will let you find me" (Jer 29:13-14). Or, in Jesus' own words, "I have come as light into the world, so that everyone who believes in me should not remain in the darkness" (John 12:46).

Nathanael's encounter with Jesus was only possible because he was an honest seeker. Philip's most important saying, and Nathanael's most important *hearing*, were: "We have found him about whom Moses in the law and also the prophets wrote" (1:45). We have found him! Messiah-recognition is crucial. Sincerity is the key to spiritual reception; it empowers one to receive revelation. The divine downreach grasps the human upreach.

Revelation utters, "what is new and what is old" (Matt 13:52). Revelation always picks up on some recognized truth and takes it further. Unfortunately, we never seem to comprehend the new revelation, so we quickly assimilate it to old ways of thinking. Humans find it almost impossible to accept new wine without pouring it into old and worn-out wineskins that are unable to stretch to hold the new and expansive truth.[5] This is nowhere more true than as regards the concept of justice. The serious and stern justice envisioned by the prior stage of evolution does not easily allow itself to be enfolded and uplifted into the mercy, spiritual repair, and progress the gospel reveals. This is not to imply that sin is insignificant or justice unnecessary, only that what is new with the gospel is not justice but God's miraculous rescue and repair operation. Yet the (human) need for justice and vindication, in this world and the next, remains. And so we have the long-standing conflict between "law" and "gospel," when really these two different emphases are both legitimate stages in revelational evolution.

The human reception of revelation always results in conflict and misunderstanding. Each revelation gets distorted as it is absorbed. Every new revelation of God has to try to reach people who have a distorted

---

[5] Mark 2:22.

understanding of the previous revelation. Tradition can even turn truth into trinkets, cheap symbols from which truth has been evacuated. The defenders of the Jewish Law had become so rigid and formalistic that Jesus had to say, "You abandon the commandment of God and hold to human tradition" (Mark 7:8). This is a *human*, not a specifically Jewish, problem. Old wineskins from which most of the new wine has leaked out are a correct metaphor for most religious institutions, and this is perhaps most visible in Christianity, since it *had* so much "new wine" to lose. Christianity has leaked more truth than any other religion. But even much of that leakage was useful, contributing, as it did, to the evolution of political philosophy in England and America. My freedom from the threat of burning as a result of writing this book is owed not only to the political rights in the U.S. Constitution but also to the teaching of Jesus that insisted on limiting the powers of Caesar. If a mere byproduct of Jesus' teachings can yield such fruit, what might happen if we enacted the core of his teachings, if we became free and responsible faith-children of God? Do we have that capacity?

6.2 Natural Theology and Growth

Alfred North Whitehead and Pierre Teilhard de Chardin articulated different forms of natural theology, the idea that God has always been working within humanity.[6] Any revelation must build on the inroads into human thought that God has already made: "revelation can only be accepted and judged as 'true' on the basis of some prior understanding of the meaning of God."[7] Unless we develop some concept of natural theology, we will produce misanthropic theologies and perpetuate cruel methods of parenting. If children are basically evil, they must be beaten, subdued, and frightened with horrifying theology such as the idea of eternal damnation. Issues of theology, ethics, and child rearing are intimately linked. We need a theology that remembers that Jesus warned against burdening or despising children.[8]

All the great thinkers of early Christianity, from Paul to Origen to Aquinas, recognized that God placed certain spiritual faculties in the human mind or personality that encourage spiritual discernment. There

---

[6] Lawrence Kohlberg, *The Philosophy of Moral Development: Moral Stages and the Idea of Justice* (San Francisco: Harper & Row, 1981) 1:367–68.

[7] Ibid., 369.

[8] Matt 18:6, 10; 19:14.

is a biblical basis for natural theology: "Truly it is the spirit in a mortal, the breath of the Almighty, that makes for understanding" (Job 32:8); "the human spirit is the lamp of the Lord" (Prov 20:27); "what can be known about God is plain to them . . . what the law requires is written on their hearts" (Rom 1:19; 2:15).

Moral and spiritual capacities were put within human nature so that we could recognize the attractions of Godly truth and goodness. Even our passionate nature seems designed to move us to "hunger and thirst for righteousness" (Matt 5:6). Revelation then comes and clarifies the messages we were receiving from our God-given spirits: the "Spirit bearing witness with our spirit that we are children of God" (Rom 8:16).

Natural theology tells us that God has implanted some faculties within us that lead us Godward; all people have the divine spark that draws their minds toward the divine. These innate faculties, however, do not provide much clarity in the way of religious *teaching*; they seem mostly to ignite spiritual desire, to foster our responsiveness to divine leading, and to provide some very simple spiritual principles. Religions as such develop the intellectual and emotional patterns of particular cultural groups. Mythic, cultic, and moral traditions then evolve. God provides a taste; humanity invents a huge and complex imaginary banquet; revelation then comes and tries to clear away some of the invented clutter and clarify what is being tasted.

The spiritual capacities are only a beginning. We also need concentrated instruction that redirects our attention to indispensable values such as impartial justice and honest worship, to essential truths such as the unity of God and the intimate approach of God to humanity in the incarnation of the Son.

One of the fundamental problems with the main atonement thinkers is that they assume simultaneously a thoroughly wicked humanity and a divine rage against these helpless sinners. They also reject natural theology, the idea that there is a Godward draw in human reason. Luther calls reason "the greatest whore that the Devil has"[9] and allows no agreement between reason and faith. "The light of nature and the light of grace cannot be friends."[10]

---

[9] Burnell F. Eckardt, Jr., *Anselm and Luther on the Atonement: Was It "Necessary"?* (San Francisco: Mellen Research University Press, 1992) 156; a different translation is in *Luther's Works* (Philadelphia: Fortress Press, 1957) 51:374, "Last Sermon in Wittenberg."

[10] Eckardt, *Anselm and Luther*, 156, quoting *Sermons of Martin Luther* 1:362.

The advancing family ethics of our time would argue against continuing to accept any doctrines, or to take literally any metaphors, that derive from an abusive parenting mentality or from methods of making satisfaction in oppressive social systems. These doctrines themselves are vestiges of the past that need to be outgrown. John Milbank places the bad atonement concepts within a continuum of religious advance and even sees them as part of what Jesus bears: "Jesus assumes the burden of these false meanings. . . . [He] allows to be incorporated into his own person ugly constructions."[11] Perhaps this is the best option with outmoded atonement concepts, to see them as a phase of childish construction that Jesus endures as he patiently waits for his children to grow up.

There must be a process whereby our knowledge of God grows, old concepts are abandoned or transformed while new ones develop, enabling us to make progress without despising our earlier stages of development. Who says we are forced to either deify or vilify the past? There is another choice besides fundamentalism or Marcionism.[12] We may begin to allow our knowledge of God to grow, "first the stalk, then the head, then the full grain in the head" (Mark 4:28). Faith is the water that keeps the plant alive, while the plant's inherent (God-given) qualities enable it to grow. Revelation is sunlight.

There is, in fact, a *growth imperative* in all aspects of life. Analogies can be drawn between the different levels because there is something similar about *life* on any level, despite the differences. On the material level "be fruitful and multiply" is a growth (reproduction) imperative. On the personal level "identify with truth and make spiritual progress" is a growth imperative or, as Jesus put it, "you will know the truth, and the truth will make you free"; "be perfect, therefore, as your heavenly Father is perfect" (John 8:32; Matt 5:48). Jesus' surprising teaching is that growth is effortless: "consider the lilies, how they grow: they neither toil nor spin," yet grow to be beautiful (Luke 12:27). He compares spiritual growth to a seed growing overnight: even while a person "would sleep . . . the seed would sprout and grow, he does not know how. The earth produces of itself" (Mark 4:27-28). Our seed-souls know how to grow if we refrain from poisoning them with dishonesty and corruption or stunting

---

[11] Milbank, *Word Made Strange*, 139, for which Horton attacks him ("Participation and Covenant," 129).

[12] Marcion, an influential second-century figure, rejected the OT and the God of Israel, as well as most of the NT. He retained only an edited version of Luke and the letters of Paul.

them with selfishness. "The whole body [of believers] . . . grows with a growth that is from God" (Col 2:19).

Once we develop an adequate hermeneutic of growth, a way of understanding progress and regression in religious ideation, we can better see how atonement ideas developed within Jewish and Greek religion, how certain formulas became compelling for a time, what social practices they resembled, and we can make more ethical, in fact more *progressive* decisions about what options are best regarding particular atonement concepts.

6.3 The Atonement Metaphor or the Family Model?

There is no denying that atonement has become entwined with many other and crucial Christian concepts, such as the divinity of Christ, the saving purpose of the Incarnation, and God's concern for humanity. If we drop atonement, do we lose all these essential ideas? Are we even tempted toward atheism? Does everything hang on the atonement, or is atonement hanging on to these other, more essential teachings? If we drop the concept of the violence of God, will we cease to believe in God at all? Is our faith a mere fiction that needs to be maintained with threats of punishment and illusions of buyout?

These questions are heavily freighted with anxieties. We must return to the response of Jesus: "Fear not, little flock, for it is your Father's good pleasure to give you the kingdom" (Luke 12:32 RSV), which undercuts the whole basis for bargaining with or persuading God through suffering and sacrifice. In what appear to be early sermons, Jesus encourages his disciples to recognize the reality of the Father's loving care for each person, which provides for growth naturally, like the overnight growth of grain, and "your heavenly Father knows that you need all these things."[13] He is "*your* heavenly Father,"[14] not just *his* Father. Jesus is always saying that the Father will give us what we need[15]—a teaching that is only meaningful if understood spiritually: in terms of desired faith, necessary perseverance, needed wisdom. The Father takes a loving father's interest in his children's welfare. This is the heart of the simple and stunning message of Jesus. This Father does not need to be appeased, made merciful, have his honor restored, or receive "satisfaction" for sin.

---

[13] Matt 6:32; cf. 6:8.

[14] Matt 6:1, 4, 6, 8, 14-15, 18, 26, 32; 7:11; 10:20, 29; 18:14; 23:9; Mark 11:25; Luke 6:36; 12:30; John 20:17; cf. Rom 8:16; 2 Cor 6:18; 1 John 3:2, emphasis added.

[15] Matt 6:33-34; 7:7-11; John 15:7; 16:23; Jas 4:3.

Rather, the mature believer must be reflective, responsible, and intelligent, and must trust that God will guide him or her in difficult decision making. "Anyone who resolves to do the will of God will know whether the teaching is from God or whether I am speaking on my own" (John 7:17). This inward training needs to be augmented by outward training and by ethical socialization; these are the church's business.

If we abandon the idea of God as judge and sacrifice demander we need to replace it with an understanding of God as parent and as director of human growth. The danger with violently discarding the atonement doctrine is that we may lose sight of the crucial truths for which it has been the vehicle: that God shares our sufferings and struggles. Christology now must continue to be the vehicle for this insight but divested of the barbaric concept of God demanding a human sacrifice. Understanding the incarnation of God in the life of Jesus remains the best way of understanding how God shares our life and continually nurtures what is good in it.

When God-trust finally displaces God-fear, the concept of the incarnation will be divested of elements of sacrifice, payoff, and atonement (that is, "atonement" in the sense of magical cleansing or manipulative payoff). There should be no problem with retaining the old English meaning: at-one-ment, becoming (gradually) united with God, but that is not what most people mean when they say "atonement."

These changes should not lead to a watering down of christology. In fact, a discerning philosophy will always lead toward christology, since there is no one who embodies "love of wisdom" as Jesus does. We need not defend christology like a besieged fortress. It is, rather, a higher ground that cannot be reached by any kind of attack. What was formerly thought to uphold christology—Jesus' death as a ransom payment or substitution—is no longer convincing and is ethically repugnant. We need to reclaim christology with greater ethical sensitivity.

Instead of saying, as Calvin did, that every person is "an heir of wrath, exposed to the curse of eternal death, excluded from all hope . . . doomed to horrible destruction" until Christ "satisfied and duly propitiated God" (*Inst.* 2.16.2), we will say that we are all children and need to grow up! We need to make adult choices and be responsible. People who do that are not depraved and utterly offensive. We are born for *growing*, not damning. If we learn to appreciate the implications of Jesus' family metaphor we will see that growth is the heart of his teaching.

If Calvin were right—if God's "hand is armed for our destruction"—we would not exist for another moment. We would be destroyed the moment God's hand became "armed" against us. Rather, "God shows his love among us" (1 John 4:9 NIV), and we can love God with our *mind* as well as with our soul. Life starts making sense when we link our scientific concept of evolution with our spiritual concept of growth. Growth is the key to life—physical and spiritual life. All of Jesus' growth images—little seed to great bush; first the grain, then the stalk, then the full ear; branches staying connected to the vine—take on new meaning. All the family imagery he uses for God's watchcare is now seen to be central to his teachings. A good Father is not a slave owner, a stern judge, or even a king, but "the Father himself loves you" (John 16:27). God planted us here in order to *grow* us. There is a fundamental contradiction between the atonement metaphor and the family metaphor—unless we are speaking of an abusive family in which the children are made to live in constant fear or to feel that they are a great burden. In both our child rearing and in our religious philosophy we should know better than that now. Recent advances in family ethics are partly the result of naturally advancing science and health care and partly the outgrowth of the values Jesus planted long ago.

6.4 Destiny and Spirituality

Revelation guides the growth and maturation of human culture and of individuals. Failure to see this leads to that dispiritedness or spiritual malaise among intellectuals that has been documented since at least the time of Dostoyevsky. Losing sight of the pattern of progress, intellectuals become increasingly downhearted. Unable to see the forest, they decide there are only trees. Without some concept of cosmic *origins, purposes,* and *destinies* data is relatively meaningless, and the more data, the more dizzying its apparent meaninglessness.

But human life is not meaningless. It does have an origin, a purpose, and a destiny—an origin both divine and natural, both spiritual and material, and a purpose and destiny that embody individual, social, and spiritual progress. The universe is a university; it is also a society; finally, it is a family. This means that we are meant to experience intellectual, social, and spiritual growth. The best analogy for illustrating much of this is also the most natural: in the family, people learn from each other; they also have to practice compromise and restraint for the sake of others; the parents are interested in enabling each child to grow intellectually, morally, and spiritually. The parents present new challenges and insights to each child according to his or her readiness.

Spirituality is the hardest of these categories to define. It is closely linked to intellectual and moral growth but is not a subset of either of those. It is also connected to the affective faculties and even to the erotic life, but it is certainly not a subset of those areas of life. Spirituality has much to do with the whole of a person's life, with the harmony and overall progress of the personality, yet it is more than just a summary of one's life. Spirit is a real level of reality, and we have Jesus' word that "God is Spirit" (John 4:24). We access that level of reality constantly. We encounter it in our interactions with other persons and again in our private reflections and creative actions; we approach it when we think about important matters in our lives, yet spirituality is not a subset of either emotion or rationality. We sense spirituality when we feel an unseen presence or are with loving people, yet spirituality is not sentimental. Thought and affection enter into our spiritual experience, but neither *is* spirituality. What of "love"? Love is easily misunderstood and its feeling aspect overemphasized, but if we understand love to entail real loyalty, not just a satisfaction of feeling, it is a good indicator of spirituality. Spirituality needs thought as much as feeling.

Defining spirit or spirituality is nearly impossible, but it can be helpful to contrast it with matter. On the strictly material level, giving means loss, but on the spiritual level, giving is gain. Materially, everything is slouching toward age, decay, and death. Spiritually, everything that identifies with truth and goodness is ascending toward permanence, for truth and discernment are the "food that endures for eternal life" (John 6:27). Jesus wants everyone to ascend: "this is the will of him who sent me, that I should lose nothing of all that he has given me, but raise it up" (John 6:39).

Doing God's will is the secret of eternal life. This bears repeating: a person becomes eternalized by identifying with the will of the Eternal. Permanence of personal existence and permanent reliability of character are the destiny of all who identify with the purposes of God. "The Lord will perfect that which concerneth me" (Ps 138:8 KJV).

The gospel affirms that the whole of creation responds to the universal mandate to seek perfection. Eternity commands time to "be perfect" (Matt 5:48), and evolution is time's response. There need be no contradiction between creational and evolutional understandings; *evolution is slow creation.* Humanity adds spiritual evolution to biologic evolution, and our closest approach to God is in our own spiritual makeup. In creating and evolving humanity, God has produced a particular kind of creature, one born an animal and becoming a spirit.

Teilhard de Chardin spoke of the gradual Christification of the human race.[16] Christ is the Omega point of evolution; he has the power "to purify, to direct and superanimate the general ascent of consciousness . . . when he has gathered everything together and transformed everything. . . . Then, as St. Paul tells us, *God shall be all in all.*"[17]

Whether or not we use Teilhard's insights, we need religious philosophy that does not see science as an enemy. Concepts of revelation without any understanding of evolution (biologic and social) now look childish and unbelievable. By the same token, the concept of evolution without divine purpose is implausible, as it cannot account for the emergence of a species that hungers for divine values. Any religious philosophy worthy of the name must offer a concept of revelation and a concept of evolution as well as a way of understanding the evolution of religion.

Everything follows evolutionary patterns, but the whole of evolution has been partly uplifted and redirected by revelation. We would like it to be uplifted again, and soon, but too-frequent intervention would violate the laws of evolution. We must allow things to be played out, "for it is proper ["fitting," NAB] for us in this way to fulfill all righteousness" (Matt 3:15). It is fitting and necessary that we learn through experience. Progress appears slow because we seem to learn only through repeated failures, finally coming to recognize that we must enact and defend certain necessary principles; we learn these lessons in the realms of religion, ethics, and government.

God is *working* on us. In fact, "as the earth brings forth its shoots, and as a garden causes what is sown in it to spring up, so the Lord GOD will cause righteousness and praise to spring up before all the nations" (Isa 61:11). This promise is at the end of the chapter Jesus chose when announcing his public ministry: "The Spirit of the Lord is upon me. . . . He has sent me to proclaim release to the captives and recovery of sight to the blind, to let the oppressed go free, to proclaim the year of the Lord's favor."[18] Isaiah 61:11 is not only the promised fulfillment of Isaiah 61:1, but also of Jesus' chosen mission statement. This is the forgotten eschatology of the Bible.

---

[16] Pierre Teilhard de Chardin, *The Divine Milieu* (New York: Harper & Row, 1960; orig. Paris: Editions du Seuil, 1957) 123–26, 154.

[17] Pierre Teilhard de Chardin, *The Phenomenon of Man* (New York: Harper & Row, 1959; orig. Paris: Editions du Seuil, 1955) 294. The biblical reference is 1 Cor 15:28. Also see Eph 1:9-10, 22.

[18] Luke 4:18-19, from Isa 61:1-2 LXX.

In one way that "favored year" was Jesus' earthly life; in another way it will take thousands of years to achieve that "year." The great promises of Isaiah and of the gospel point to this day of consummation, when finally there will be "faith on earth" (Luke 18:8). How long will it take before "the earth will be full of the knowledge of the LORD as the waters cover the sea" (Isa 11:9; Hab 2:14)? It will require ages-long and persistent human cooperation.

Sincerity is the key to progress, as it empowers one to receive revelation. The divine downreach yearns after a receptive human upreach. It takes two to tango. "Let justice descend, O heavens, like dew from above. . . . Let the earth open and salvation bud forth" (Isa 45:8 NAB). All our earthly struggles would be meaningless if they yielded no real advance, if perfection were to be imposed from on high without our participation. Only with human cooperation will the promise be fulfilled; then "faithfulness will spring up from the ground, and righteousness will look down from the sky" (Ps 85:11).

We do not effortlessly evolve toward our Deity destiny; we need to develop self-mastery, scientific advance, and progress in the culture of child rearing. We must beware of regression, of anger-motivated solutions that are no solution. But woe to us if we give up the struggle! Either we are being transformed into the likeness of God, or else we are becoming more "bestial" than any beast.

I have constructed this narrative of hope as part of my project of suggesting that we might rethink salvation in terms of Jesus' family metaphor, in which the Father is concerned to take care of his children and constant growth is taking place "from one degree of glory to another" (2 Cor 3:18) rather than in terms of atonement metaphors that suggest ritual manipulation, ransom payment, and the criminal law court. Because of the harshness of these human institutions these images need to be replaced with ones that are consistent with the parental watchful care of God, and the old, vindictive eschatology needs to be replaced with the hope-filled eschatology of the passages quoted above.

It seems that fear-based concepts of salvation were a necessary stepping-stone in the evolution of religion, but Jesus offered trust in place of fear (Luke 8:50; 12:32), something that was evidently too radical (or too unstructured?) even for the church, which before long reverted to familiar authoritarian structures and antique ideas of retribution, in which humanity was only rescued from savage retribution through the performance of a ritual murder. If a sacrifice had to be provided before God could act on his own intention to forgive, this makes God subject to a supposedly implacable law of retribution and sacrifice. It overlooks Jesus' *own* method of extending forgiveness: "When Jesus saw their faith, he said to the paralytic, 'Son, your sins are forgiven'" (Mark 2:5); "Friend, your sins are forgiven you" (Luke 5:20). The message is a healing one: "your faith has made you well" (Matt 9:22; Mark 5:34; 10:52; Luke 8:48); "the Father himself loves you" (John 16:27). There is no transaction here.

But this does not mean that the individual's faith is all-powerful, independent of Christ or of grace. Faith is faith *in Jesus*:

> "Do you believe that I am able to do this?" They said to him, "Yes, Lord." Then he touched their eyes and said, "According to your faith let it be done to you." And their eyes were opened. (Matt 9:28-30)

Bibliography

Primary Sources

Anselm. *Cur Deus Homo?* Two sources used:

Cur Deus Homo? Translated by Edward S. Prout. London: Religious Tract Society, 1887.

Eckardt, Burnell F. Jr. *Anselm and Luther on the Atonement: Was It "Necessary"?* San Francisco: Mellen Research University Press, 1992.

Augustine. Several works, several sources:

Enarrationes in Psalmos and *Contra Faustum*. From Eugène Portalie, ed., *Guide to the Thought of Saint Augustine*. Translated by Ralph Bastian. Chicago: Henry Regnery, 1960.

The Enchiridion on Faith, Hope and Love. Translated by Henry Paolucci. Chicago: Henry Regnery, 1961.

Calvin, Jean. *Institutes of the Christian Religion*. Translated by Henry Beveridge. Grand Rapids: Eerdmans, 1975.

Euripides. *Ten Plays by Euripides*. Translated by Moses Hadas and John McLean. New York: Bantam Books, 1960.

Gregory the Great. Morals of Job:

Cory, Catherine A., and David T. Landry, eds., *The Christian Theological Tradition*. Englewood Cliffs, NJ: Prentice-Hall, 2000.

Dudden, F. Homes. *Gregory the Great: His Place in History and Thought, vol. II*. New York: Longmans, Green, 1905.

Gregory of Nazianzus. Fifth Theological Oration: "On the Holy Spirit": *Nicene and Post-Nicene Fathers of the Christian Church*, second series (NPNF 2). Edited by Philip Schaff and Henry Wace. Grand Rapids: Eerdmans, 1983.

Ignatius of Antioch. *Early Christian Writings*. Revised translation by Andrew Louth. London: Penguin, 1968.

Luther, Martin. For various works, three sources used:

Dillenberger, John, ed., *Martin Luther: Selections from His Writings*. Garden City, NY: Doubleday, 1961.

Eckardt, *Anselm and Luther on the Atonement*.

The Sermons of Martin Luther, vol. 7. Grand Rapids: Baker, 1988.

Sophocles. *Sophocles: The Theban Plays*. Translated by E. F. Watling. London: Penguin Books, 1947.

Secondary Sources

Attridge, Harold W. *The Epistle to the Hebrews*. Hermeneia. Philadelphia: Fortress Press, 1989.

Bailey, Daniel P. "Jesus as the Mercy Seat: The Semantics and Theology of Paul's Use of *Hilastērion* in Romans 3:25." Ph.D. diss., Cambridge University, 1999.

Bainton, Roland H. *The Travail of Religious Liberty*. New York: Harper & Brothers, 1951.

Balentine, Samuel E. *Leviticus*. Interpretation. Louisville: Westminster John Knox, 2002.

Balthasar, Hans Urs von. *Theo-Drama: Theological Dramatical Theory*. Volume 4: *The Action*. San Francisco: Ignatius Press, 1994.

Beier, Matthias. *A Violent God-Image: An Introduction to the Work of Eugen Drewermann*. New York: Continuum, 2004.

Bockmuehl, Markus. *Revelation and Mystery in Ancient Judaism and Pauline Christianity*. Grand Rapids: Eerdmans, 1997.

Boersma, Hans. "Being Reconciled: Atonement as the Ecclesio-Christological Practice of Forgiveness in John Milbank," in James K. A. Smith and James H. Olthuis, eds., *Radical Orthodoxy and the Reformed Tradition: Creation, Covenant, and Participation*. Grand Rapids: Baker Academic, 2005, 183–202

———. *Violence, Hospitality, and the Cross*. Grand Rapids: Baker, 2004.

Borg, Marcus J. *Meeting Jesus Again for the First Time*. San Francisco: HarperSanFrancisco, 1994.

Bradley, Ian. *Power of Sacrifice*. London: Darton Longman and Todd, 1995.

Bultmann, Rudolf. *Theology of the New Testament*. Vol. 1. New York: Charles Scribner's Sons, 1951.

Burke, Kenneth. *Permanence and Change: An Anatomy of Purpose*. Rev. ed. Los Altos, CA: Hermes, 1954.

Capps, Donald. *The Child's Song: The Religious Abuse of Children*. Louisville: Westminster John Knox, 1995.

Chaplin, Jonathan. "Suspended Communities or Covenant Communities? Reformed Reflections on the Social Thought of Radical Orthodoxy," in James K. A. Smith and James H. Olthuis, eds., *Radical Orthodoxy and the Reformed Tradition: Creation, Covenant, and Participation*. Grand Rapids: Baker Academic, 2005, 151–82.

Christensen, Michael, ed. *Partakers of the Divine Nature: The History and Development of Deification in the Christian Traditions*. Madison, NJ: Fairleigh Dickinson University Press, 2006.

Comstock, Richard W. *The Study of Religion and Primitive Religions*. New York: Harper & Row, 1971.

Dennis, John. "The Function of the *ḥṭ'ṭ* Sacrifice in the Priestly Literature," *ETL* 78 (2002) 108–29.

de Silva, David A. *Despising Shame: Honor Discourse and Community Maintenance in the Epistle to the Hebrews*. SBLDS 152. Atlanta: Scholars Press, 1995.

Duncan, Hugh Dalziel. *Symbols and Social Theory*. New York: Oxford University Press, 1969.

Dundes, Alan. "The Ritual Murder or Blood Libel Legend," in idem, ed., *The Blood Libel Legend: A Casebook in Anti-Semitic Folklore*. Madison: University of Wisconsin Press, 1991, 336–76.

Dunn, James D. G. *The Theology of Paul the Apostle*. Grand Rapids: Eerdmans, 1998.

Eckardt, Burnell F. Jr. *Anselm and Luther on the Atonement: Was It "Necessary"?* San Francisco: Mellen Research University Press, 1992.

Ehrman, Bart D. *The Orthodox Corruption of Scripture: The Effect of Early Christological Controversies on the Text of the New Testament*. Oxford: Oxford University Press, 1993.

Fiddes, Paul S. *Past Event and Present Salvation: The Christian Idea of Atonement*. Louisville: Westminster John Knox, 1989.

Finlan, Stephen. *The Background and Content of Paul's Cultic Atonement Metaphors*. Ac Bib 19. Atlanta: SBL/Brill, 2004.

———. *Problems with Atonement: The Origins of, and Controversy about, the Atonement Doctrine*. Collegeville, MN: Liturgical Press, 2005.

Finlan, Stephen, and Vladimir Kharlamov, eds. *Theosis: Deification in Christian Tradition*. PTMS 52. Eugene, OR: Wipf & Stock, 2006.

Girard, René. *I See Satan Fall Like Lightning*. Trans. James G. Williams. Maryknoll, NY: Orbis, 2001.

———. *Things Hidden Since the Foundation of the World*. London: Athlone, 1987.

Goodspeed, Edgar J. "Some Greek Notes," *JBL* 73 (1954) 84–92.

Gorman, Frank H. Jr. *The Ideology of Ritual: Space, Time and Status in the Priestly Theology*. JSOTSup 91. Sheffield: Sheffield Academic Press, 1990.

Gorringe, Timothy. *God's Just Vengeance: Crime, Violence and the Rhetoric of Salvation*. Cambridge Studies in Ideology and Religion 9. Cambridge: Cambridge University Press, 1996.

———. "Title and Metaphor in Christology," *ExpT* 95 (1983–84) 8–12.

Gray, George Buchanan. *Sacrifice in the Old Testament: Its Theory and Practice*. Oxford: Clarendon Press, 1925.

Gunton, Colin E. *The Actuality of Atonement: A Study of Metaphor, Rationality and the Christian Tradition*. Grand Rapids: Eerdmans, 1989.

———. "Christ the Sacrifice: Aspects of the Language and Imagery of the Bible," in idem, *The Glory of Christ in the New Testament: Studies in Christology*. Oxford: Clarendon Press, 1987, 229–38.

———. "Towards a Theology of Reconciliation," in idem, ed., *The Theology of Reconciliation*. London: T & T Clark, 2003, 167–74.

Hardin, Michael. "Sacrificial Language in Hebrews: Reappraising René Girard," in Willard M. Swartley, ed., *Violence Renounced: René Girard, Biblical Studies, and Peacemaking*. Telford, PA: Telford Press, 2000, 103–19.

Hare, Douglas A. *The Son of Man Tradition*. Minneapolis: Fortress Press, 1990.

Hedley, Douglas. "Should Divinity Overcome Metaphysics? Reflections on John Milbank's Theology beyond Secular Reason and Confessions of a Cambridge Platonist," *JR* 80 (2000) 271–98.

Heesterman, J. C. *The Inner Conflict of Tradition: Essays in Indian Ritual, Kingship, and Society.* Chicago: University of Chicago Press, 1985.

Heyer, C. J. den. *Jesus and the Doctrine of Atonement: Biblical Notes on a Controversial Topic.* London: SCM, 1998.

Holladay, William L. *A Concise Hebrew and Aramaic Lexicon of the Old Testament.* Grand Rapids: Eerdmans, 1988.

Holmes, Colin. "The Ritual Murder Accusation in Britain," in Alan Dundes, ed., *The Blood Libel Legend: A Casebook in Anti-Semitic Folklore.* Madison: University of Wisconsin Press, 1991, 99–134.

Holmes, Steve. "Can Punishment Bring Peace? Penal Substitution Revisited," *SJT* 58 (2005) 104–23.

Horton, Michael S. "Participation and Covenant," in James K. A. Smith and James H. Olthuis, eds., *Radical Orthodoxy and the Reformed Tradition: Creation, Covenant, and Participation.* Grand Rapids: Baker Academic, 2005, 107–32.

Hsia, R. po-chia. *The Myth of Ritual Murder.* New Haven: Yale University Press, 1988.

Hunter, Archibald M. *Interpreting Paul's Gospel.* London: SCM, 1954.

Johns, Loren L. "'A Better Sacrifice' or 'Better Than Sacrifice'? Response to Hardin's 'Sacrificial Language in Hebrews,'" in Willard M. Swartley, ed., *Violence Renounced: René Girard, Biblical Studies, and Peacemaking.* Telford, PA: Telford Press, 2000, 120–31.

Knohl, Israel. "The Sin Offering Law in the 'Holiness School,'" in Gary A. Anderson and Saul M. Olyan, eds., *Priesthood and Cult in Ancient Israel.* JSOTSup 125. Sheffield: Sheffield Academic Press, 1991, 192–203.

Kodell, Jerome. *Sin, Salvation, and the Spirit.* Collegeville, MN: Liturgical Press, 1979.

Kohlberg, Lawrence. *The Philosophy of Moral Development: Moral Stages and the Idea of Justice.* San Francisco: Harper & Row, 1981.

Kuula, Kari. *The Law, the Covenant and God's Plan,* Vol. 2 of *Paul's Treatment of the Law and Israel in Romans.* Göttingen: Vandenhoeck & Ruprecht, 2003.

Marshall, Christopher D. *Beyond Retribution: A New Testament Vision for Justice, Crime, and Punishment.* Grand Rapids: Eerdmans, 2001.

Milbank, John. *Being Reconciled: Ontology and Pardon.* Radical Orthodoxy Series. London: Routledge, 2003.

———. "Stories of Sacrifice," *Modern Theology* 12 (1996) 27–56.

———. *The Word Made Strange: Theology, Language, Culture.* Oxford: Blackwell, 1997.

Milgrom, Jacob. *Leviticus 1–16.* AB 3. Garden City, NY: Doubleday, 1991.

———. *Leviticus 17–22.* AB 3A. Garden City, NY: Doubleday, 2000.

———. "The Priestly Laws of Sancta Contamination," in Michael Fishbane and Emanuel Tov, eds., *"Sha'arei Talmon": Studies in the Bible, Qumran, and the*

Ancient Near East Presented to Shemaryahu Talmon. Winona Lake: Eisenbrauns, 1992, 137–46.

Miller, Alice. *Banished Knowledge: Facing Childhood Injuries.* New York: Doubleday, 1990.

Morris, Leon. *The Apostolic Preaching of the Cross.* 3rd rev. ed. Grand Rapids: Eerdmans, 1965.

Moule, C. F. D. *Essays in New Testament Interpretation.* Cambridge: Cambridge University Press, 1982.

———. "Preaching the Atonement," *Epworth Review* 10/2 (1983) 70–78.

———. *The Sacrifice of Christ.* FBBS 12. Philadelphia: Fortress Press, 1964.

———. "The Theology of Forgiveness," in Norman Autton, ed., *From Fear to Faith: Studies of Suffering and Wholeness.* London: S.P.C.K., 1971, 61–72.

Nelson-Pallmeyer, Jack. *Is Religion Killing Us? Violence in the Bible and the Quran.* Harrisburg: Trinity Press International, 2003.

———. *Jesus Against Christianity: Reclaiming the Missing Jesus.* Harrisburg: Trinity Press International, 2001.

Odell-Scott, David W. *A Post-Patriarchal Christology.* AARA 78. Atlanta: Scholars Press, 1991.

Parke, James. *The Conflict of the Church and Synagogue.* Cleveland and New York: World, 1961.

Perkins, Pheme. "God, Cosmos and Church Universal: The Theology of Ephesians," *SBLSP* 2000. Atlanta: Scholars Press, 2000, 752–73.

Placher, William C. *Jesus the Savior: The Meaning of Jesus Christ for Christian Faith.* Louisville: Westminster John Knox, 2001.

Poliakov, Léon. *The History of Anti-Semitism.* Trans. Richard Howard. New York: Vanguard, 1965.

Rahner, Karl. *Foundations of Christian Faith: An Introduction to the Idea of Christianity.* Trans. William Dych. New York: Seabury, 1978.

Rappaport, Ernest A. "The Ritual Murder Accusation: The Persistence of Doubt and the Repetition Compulsion," in Alan Dundes, ed., *The Blood Libel Legend: A Casebook in Anti-Semitic Folklore.* Madison: University of Wisconsin Press, 1991, 304–35.

Russell, Norman. *The Doctrine of Deification in the Greek Patristic Tradition.* Oxford: Oxford University Press, 2005.

Safanov, Anatol. "Blood Accusation," in Isaac Landman, ed., *The Universal Jewish Encyclopedia.* New York: The Universal Jewish Encyclopedia, 1940, 407–10.

Samuel, Maurice. *The Great Hatred.* New York: Knopf, 1940.

Schmiechen, Peter. *Saving Power: Theories of Atonement and Forms of the Church.* Grand Rapids: Eerdmans, 2005.

Schwager, Raymund. *Jesus in the Drama of Salvation: Toward a Biblical Doctrine of Redemption.* Trans. James G. Williams and Paul Haddon. New York: Crossroad, 1999.

———. *Must There Be Scapegoats? Violence and Redemption in the Bible.* New York: Crossroad, 2000.

Schwöbel, Christoph. "Reconciliation: From Biblical Observations to Dogmatic Reconstruction," in Colin E. Gunton, ed., *The Theology of Reconciliation*. London: T & T Clark, 2003.

Smith, Brian K. *Reflections on Resemblance, Ritual, and Religion*. Oxford: Oxford University Press, 1989.

Snodgrass, Klyne. "The Gospel of Jesus," in Markus Bockmuehl and Donald A. Hagner, eds., *The Written Gospel*. Cambridge: Cambridge University Press, 2005, 31–44.

Stählin, Gustav. περίπσημα, *TDNT* 6:84–93.

Stökl Ben Ezra, Daniel. *The Impact of Yom Kippur on Early Christianity: The Day of Atonement from Second Temple Judaism to the Fifth Century*. WUNT 163. Tübingen: Mohr, 2003.

Stowers, Stanley K. *A Rereading of Romans: Justice, Jews, and Gentiles*. New Haven: Yale University Press, 1994.

Straw, Carole. *Gregory the Great: Perfection in Imperfection*. Transformation of the Classical Heritage 14. Berkeley: University of California Press, 1988.

Stuhlmacher, Peter. *Paul's Letter to the Romans: A Commentary*. Louisville: Westminster John Knox, 1994.

Teilhard de Chardin, Pierre. *The Divine Milieu*. New York: Harper & Row, 1960; orig. Paris, 1957.

———. *The Phenomenon of Man*. New York: Harper & Row, 1959; orig. Paris: Editions du Seuil, 1955.

Tillich, Paul. *A History of Christian Thought from Its Judaic and Hellenistic Origins to Existentialism*. New York: Simon and Schuster, 1967.

Trachtenberg, Joshua. *The Devil and the Jews*. New Haven: Yale University Press, 1943.

Van Henten, Jan Willem. *The Maccabean Martyrs as Saviours of the Jewish People: A Study of 2 and 4 Maccabees*. JSJSup 57. Leiden: Brill, 1997.

Westcott, B. F., and F. J. A. Hort. *Introduction to the New Testament in the Original Greek with Notes on Selected Readings*. Peabody, MA: Hendrickson, 1988, from the original 1882 edition.

Wheeler, David L. *A Relational View of the Atonement: Prolegomenon to a Reconstruction of the Doctrine*. AUS Series 7, Theology and Religion 54. New York: Peter Lang, 1989.

Williams, Charles. *Arthurian Torso*. Oxford: Oxford University Press, 1948.

Williams, James G. *The Bible, Violence, and the Sacred: Liberation from the Myth of Sanctioned Violence*. San Francisco: HarperSanFrancisco, 1991.

Williams, Patricia A. *Doing without Adam and Eve: Sociobiology and Original Sin*. Theology and the Sciences. Minneapolis: Fortress Press, 2001.

Wink, Walter. *The Powers That Be: Theology for a New Millennium*. New York: Doubleday, 1998.

Young, Frances M. *The Use of Sacrificial Ideas in Greek Christian Writers from the New Testament to John Chrysostom*. Patristic Monograph Series 2. Eugene, OR: Wipf & Stock, 1979.

Index of Modern Authors

Index of Ancient Texts

in Roman Catholic Canonical Order